# COMPUTER NETWORK

## NETWORK+
## CERTIFICATION STUDY GUIDE FOR
## N10-008 EXAM

## 2 BOOKS IN 1

**BOOK 1**
BEGINNERS GUIDE TO NETWORK FUNDAMENTALS AND PROTOCOLS
**BOOK 2**
BEGINNERS GUIDE TO ENTERPRISE NETWORK INFRASTRUCTURE FUNDAMENTALS

## BEGINNERS GUIDE TO NETWORK FUNDAMENTALS, PROTOCOLS & ENTERPRISE NETWORK INFRASTRUCTURE

# RICHIE MILLER

## Disclaimer

Every effort was made to produce this book as truthful as possible, but no warranty is implied. The author shall have neither liability nor responsibility to any person or entity concerning any loss or damages ascending from the information contained in this book. The information in the following pages are broadly considered to be truthful and accurate of facts, and such any negligence, use or misuse of the information in question by the reader will render any resulting actions solely under their purview.

## Table of Contents – Book 1

## Table of Contents – Book 2

# BOOK 1

# COMPUTER NETWORKING:

## NETWORK+ CERTIFICATION STUDY GUIDE FOR N10-008 EXAM

## BEGINNERS GUIDE TO
## NETWORK FUNDAMENTALS AND PROTOCOLS

### RICHIE MILLER

# Introduction

The Network+ credential is the first certification that many IT professionals ever receive. It has been around for over 25 years at this point and has been awarded to over a million applicants during that time and this matter, because the certification has become well known by IT employers. When you're looking for a job and you have the Network+ after your name, most companies know that that's a real credential. It's also a vendor-neutral credential, in the sense that it doesn't promote any particular hardware or software vendor and although the exams do recognize and reflect the prominence of Microsoft Windows in the corporate world, they also include limited content on Apple operating systems, Linux, Android, and Chrome OS. Because Apple's operating systems only run on Apple hardware, the exams do cover Macs, iPhones, and iPads. It's fair to say that the CompTIA Network+ exams try to reflect the hardware and software that a technical support professional is likely to see in real life, and that's part of its relevance and appeal. In a nutshell, the Network+ certification is the preferred performance-based qualifying credential for technical support and IT operational roles, according to the organization that manages it, CompTIA. The Network+ certification focuses on the day-to-day work of an IT technician in a business environment. One reason the Network+ certification receives respect by IT employers is that it is accredited by international organizations. The ISO, or International Standards Organization, is a worldwide standard-setting group headquartered in Geneva, and ANSI, the American National Standards Institute, is the USA's representative to ISO. CompTIA has been accredited by ANSI for compliance with the ISO standard that applies to operating a certification body or organization, and CompTIA must maintain certain quality levels in order to maintain that accreditation. That's a bit of background on CompTIA and the Network+ certification. But who might benefit from this credential? Well, anyone wanting to be hired on by a company that requires it, certainly, but more broadly, anybody pursuing a career in tech support, for example, as a help desk analyst, service desk analyst or a desktop support technician. Field service techs will also find the credential helpful, as will those who aspire to being a network engineer or a documentation specialist in IT. This book will help you prepare for the latest CompTIA Network+ Certification, exam code: N10-008. First you will discover what the most important Network Concepts and network Protocols and what can you expect from the CompTIA Network+ Exam. Next you will discover what is the OSI Model and how Encapsulation works. After that, you will learn about essential Port Numbers, TCP, UDP and SQL Database Protocols, as well as DHCP, DNS and NTP. Next you will discover what are both Binary and Hexadecimal Numbers and how to convert Decimal numbers to Binary numbers. After that we will cover IPv4 Addressing Fundamentals as well as Classless and

Classfull Addressing. You will also learn about IP Address Types and how to Subnet IPv4 Networks. Moving on, we will over IPv6 Address Fundamentals and how IPv6 SLAAC and IPv6 DHCP works. Next, you will discover how NAT or Network Address Translation works, as well as the Dynamic Host Configuration Protocol and the Domain Name System. As you can see, this book is a comprehensive guide on the CompTIA Network+ Certification and will reveal the must-have skills that every IT pro has. By finishing this book, you will become an IT professional, nevertheless, it is recommended to read the book or listen the audiobook several times to follow the provided guide. The audiobook listeners will receive a complementary PDF document, containing over 70 images; hence it's also advantageous to highlight critical subjects to review them later using a paperback or hardcover book, or the accompanied PDF once printed out for your reference. If you are a complete beginner, having limited knowledge or no experience and want to speed up your IT skills, this book will provide a tremendous amount of value to you! If you already working in IT but you want to learn the latest standards, this book will be extremely useful to you. If you want to pass the CompTIA Network+ Certification Exam fast, let's first cover some basic network concepts and network protocols!

## Chapter 1 Network Concepts and Protocols

This is the first book of four that will help prepare you for the CompTIA Network+ N10-008 exam. We're going to do is introduce networking, talk about all of the critical terminology, and make sure you walk away from this book and the rest of them with a really solid understanding of data networks so that you can use that to both better your career or help understand what's happening inside of a data network better. First we are going to define what data networking is so that you understand the fundamentals and then we will cover communication processes. But what is data networking? In the simplest sense, if you've never really thought about what data is networking before, you might think of data networking as these devices in your house.

These are cable modems. It could be a DSL modem; it could be a fiber optic modem. But typically anybody that has an internet connection is likely to have one of these devices in their house that they use to connect to the internet. You might think of data networking as these devices.

You likely have a device that looks similar to this as well. This is a wireless router, and this allows your smartphone, tablets, laptops, or other devices to communicate with the internet as well. However, networking is much bigger than just those home devices. Inside of a data center or a business or a networking closet, you may see some switches like this with lots of bundles of cables plugging into these devices in order to provide network connectivity.

Not all of them are nice and neat and pretty like this one. Some of them get a lot messier, like this one here, where it's just a bird's nest of wires.

But both of these systems are doing the exact same thing, which is to provide networking to devices, typically, in this case in an office. Now that we've seen some devices and equipment that look like data networking, let's talk more about what it actually is because that's just the gear to facilitate it. Data networking is actually more about transferring information. A server typically is connected to a network, and servers then hold data. And on a particular server, I'm imagining, is the Wikipedia server, which contains an article on computer networks. What I want to do as an end user is I want to go onto my PC, type in wikipedia.org, and then do a search for computer networks. I do that, and what I end up doing is, I connect through the network which I've represented as a cloud. And from this point forward, anytime we see a cloud icon, that means that there is some data network involved there. There's a bunch of switches and routers and wires and fiber optics and wireless that are all working together to transfer this information. I represent it with a cloud because it's much simpler when we're just trying to focus on certain aspects of this process. I go on my computer, I search for that Wikipedia article, it gets to the Wikipedia server, and then the server transfers it to my computer so I can then read it. This really is what data networking is all about. It's some version of this exact process. So what is data networking? It's a system of hardware, software, and protocols used to move information from one device to another. This is really what data networking is. It's about moving information with a very specific set of software, hardware, and protocols. But let's introduce data networking and some of the processes we use here by talking about something that we do relatively often, maybe not as often as we once did. Now we usually are texting our friends versus calling them, but let's just say here that in this example we have Anna with her smartphone, and she wants to call her friend Bob to ask him for help. Well, in order to do that, there's all kinds of processes that are happening in order to facilitate this, but if we think about it in some very simple terms, in order for her to contact Bob and ask him for help, she has to go on her smartphone, open up the phone app, find Bob's contact, click on it. That will allow his phone to ring, he will answer and say hello, she'll say hello, and now Anna can ask for some help. What's going to happen here is Anna is going to start talking, and when she talks, that's going to vibrate the air. And that vibrating air is what carries our voice. If Bob we're just sitting right next to Anna, he could just sit and listen to the air vibrate his own eardrum, and there would be no need for any other equipment. However, since he's on the other end of this phone, what's going to happen is, Anna's voice is going to vibrate the microphone on her phone. There's a little membrane in the microphone. It's going to vibrate that membrane, which is going to create a little electrical signal inside the phone. What the phone will do then is it'll take that electrical signal, and it will convert it into a wireless signal that it can send up to the cell tower. Then the cell tower takes that wireless signal, and it's going to convert it again. So now Anna's voice was encoded in this wireless signal. That encoded voice is then going to get translated into a signal that can travel across the wires on the telephone poles. They might be fiber optic; they might be copper. But we can send that signal from one cell tower to another cell tower over that system. The next cell tower that's closest to Bob's phone will then convert that signal that came in over the wire back to a wireless signal, send that down to his phone. That signal will then get translated in his phone to some electrical pulses that vibrate the membrane of a speaker. That membrane vibrates the air and then Bob can hear those vibrations as Anna's voice asking for help. So when we're using our cell phones to communicate with each other, it's this constant process of translating our message from one type of signal to another type of signal to another type of signal without ever actually losing the data that we're trying to send. This right here is a very oversimplified version of what we're doing in data networking. Data networking does the same thing. We take messages, we encapsulate them inside of virtual envelopes, and then we send those envelopes across multiple different types of network, where they get translated again and again and again. We're going to look at that throughout this entire series of books, but all the terminology, language, protocols, and systems that are used in order to make that happen.

## Chapter 2 CompTIA Network+ Exam Information

Here we're going to take a look at some exam objectives. If you're not studying for the Network+ certification exam, no problem. Skip to the next chapter. If you are studying for this, what you may want to do is go and download the exam objectives at this website. You can go to certification.comptia.org/certifications/network, and that will give you a list of the certification exam objectives. This is all the details of everything covered on that exam. It is broken into five domains, networking fundamentals, network implementations, network operations, network security, and network troubleshooting.

| | |
|---|---|
| 1.0 Networking Fundamentals | 24% |
| 2.0 Network Implementations | 19% |
| 3.0 Network Operations | 16% |
| 4.0 Network Security | 19% |
| 5.0 Network Troubleshooting | 22% |
| **Total** | **100%** |

The books that we have designed to prepare you for the certification are generally broken up exactly into the domains that you see here, with the exception of a few topics. If we go download these objectives, it comes in a somewhat lengthy document. They have information about the exam. Then they go through each domain and they break down exactly what you need to know. This document is very thorough, very lengthy, and it covers all of the topics that you're going to need to know about. As we go through the book, you're going to learn about each one of these little snippets of information. It even has an acronym list at the end because there are tons of acronyms to learn in data networking. There's also hardware and software they talk about as well. You can download this document for yourself and review it. As you're learning the exam, you can actually use this to check off the stuff that you feel like you know and the stuff that you need more help with. In summary we have defined what is networking. We looked at communication processes to see how a cell phone call to our friend transfers the encoded signal of our voice across multiple different media to reach our other friend's phone and then we looked at the CompTIA Network+ exam objectives. Next we are going to look at modeling data networking so that we have a very precise system to understand the order of operations in data networks.

# Chapter 3 OSI Model & Network Operations

In this chapter, we're going to be using the OSI model to describe network operations. Our goal here is going to be to introduce the OSI model to identify the very specific components of network communication. Also, remind ourselves about that telephone call between Anna and Bob, and then use that to jump into modeling networking with the OSI model. The OSI model stands for Open Systems Interconnect. It's a model that was developed in the 70s in order to describe network operation. There's lots of different protocols involved in data networking, and what the OSI model did is it gave us a place to categorize each of these protocols, as well as give the exact order that those protocols need to be processed in. If you remember this phone call I talked about previously, the order of operations here were such that Anna had to vibrate the air, which vibrated the microphone, which converted it into electrical signals, which then got converted into wireless signals, which got converted into a different type of electrical signal, and so on, until that message reached Bob on the other side. In order for that to happen, there is a very precise set of rules that need to happen and protocols that need to be followed in order for this conversation to successfully happen. When we're working with data networking, it's almost exactly the same; we just have these different components involved versus our smartphones and our voice. We're going to be using a computer or a tablet or a smartphone, like maybe an internet browser on a smartphone, to do our communication. We have a PC. This is our end-user device. Sometimes this is called a client, sometimes it's called a workstation, PC. That's the device we're going to be using to surf the web. Another device in our network, especially in our home network, is likely going to be a wireless router device. We can then connect our PC up to that wireless router. That router typically has some switchports on the back, so we can actually plug in a cable to that. Or we might be using it as a wireless device and actually not have any cables at all and just use the wireless communication to communicate between our workstation and the wireless access point. In order to get access to the internet, we need some type of device to bridge the network connection between our wireless access point and the internet, and that's where a modem comes in. So we're slowly building this network up. Then out on the internet, we have a bunch of servers out on the internet. This is going to be the servers that contain all of the information that we are going to transfer from the server to our workstation so that we can read the news, surf Facebook or other social media, or maybe check our email. For the purposes of this, I'm going to avoid the wireless for this moment. We're going to come back and talk lots more about wireless in the future. But for now, I'm just going to connect my workstation to our network with a cable. Now we have this basic network. Remember before I said that cloud represents a bunch of devices and protocols that we don't want to represent individually? And that's exactly what I'm doing here as well. That internet now is a cloud. It's thousands of devices that we're going to use to connect to our server to transfer information. Let's say that on my workstation I want to go to google.com. So I type that into my browser, and that's going to send a message to the Google server. The Google server is then going to grab the website that we're looking for, it's going to put that into a message, and then send it over to my workstation so that I can browse the videos on Google. In order for that to happen, we need a very specific set of rules and orders of operations. If you start with the most basic things that we can see, we can see the cables that we're using. The cables don't have any special electronics in them, or at least most of them don't. They're typically just some wires with a special connector on the end so that we can plug them into things. But there's no special electronics in those devices. Those cables do follow protocols though. So the Ethernet cable that we use to connect our computer to our wireless access point there, or our switch, that cable follows a very precise set of rules on how it's constructed. It just doesn't have anything electronic in it. All these cables that we have are used to connect things together. There's even wireless cables. That might be our wireless connection in our home from our smartphone to the wireless access point. Or even out on the internet, there might be some connections that use a point-to-point wireless connection. These are also cables, in that they're used to transfer information, they follow a specific protocol, but it's not a device. It's actually the signal itself that we're talking about here. In the case of the cables that connect our workstations together, these are called twisted pair cables. These twisted pair cables follow a very specific set of rules, which we'll learn about later. Oftentimes connecting our server to the rest of the network we're going to use twisted pair cabling. Connecting our cable modem to the internet might use a coax cable. Then out on the internet, we're likely going to be using fiber optics, or very thin strands of glass, in order to transfer our information. All of these cables, these different cables, whether it be wireless, twisted pair, coax, fiber optics, are technology that we use in order to transfer our data from one device to another. All of this stuff is happening at what we call the physical layer of the OSI model. The physical layer is also layer 1, and the physical layer is really what we're talking about when we're talking about cables, specifications for cables, whether that be wireless, copper, or glass. The next layer of the OSI model is going to be used to have protocols that allow us to transfer bits of information over the cables. There is a specific protocol called Ethernet that we use to transfer data from our workstation to the wireless router, from the wireless router to the cable modem, from the cable modem to wherever our internet provider is, from the server to our switches inside of our data center, and then numerous other protocols on the internet used to transfer information. All those are representing different protocols that could be used to transfer data and each one of these protocols is a little bit different, but they work together all at the same level. The connection between my PC and the router, the router and the cable modem, and then the server and the rest of the internet, that's likely using Ethernet. The connection between our cable modem and the rest of the internet is likely using a protocol called DOCSIS 3. Out on the internet it's mainly Ethernet, but there could be other protocols out there. All of these protocols, Ethernet, DOCSIS, are all part of the data link layer, and they provide all of the structure to be able to use the cables that are connected to it. They provide the protocols and the rules, specifications for electronics, as well as how to create and move a message across those links. So that's layer 2 of our OSI model, is the data link layer. The data link layer is facilitating communication. It's allowing us to pass data from one device to another. However, if I want to send a message to a device that's far away, that's not on my little local network, what I need to do is I need some other mechanism to do that. So I need another type of protocol in order to do this, so I might need to communicate between my PC and my cable modem, or I might need to communicate from the cable modem out to the internet someplace, or I might need to communicate, in this case, I will need to communicate, from my workstation all the way to Google servers and back again. So I need some way of sending a message from my workstation to Google and then getting it back, and this is where we use a protocol called Internet Protocol, and we use something called IP addressing. The IP addressing allows us as users to communicate with nearly any device on the internet. This is where IP addressing occurs, IP routing, and it is all the network layer, which is layer 3 of our OSI model.

So far we have the physical layer, our cables, we have the data link layer, which are the protocols that allow our computer and other devices to communicate locally with other devices. Then we have layer 3, the network layer. That allows us to make use of the data link layer and physical layer to send messages long distances across a network. The next layer we're going to talk about is, in order for us to have a conversation between our client, or workstation, and our server, where Google.com's website is hosted, and we need a way to build a session in between these two devices so that they can send information between each other and understand that the conversation is meant for specific things in that network communication. But for now, let's go back to our cell phone example here, where we're making a phone call. We talked about kind of like the vibrating air and whatnot with this, but more so there's another way to look at this conversation. There's another protocol we follow in order to make this conversation work. I can't just pick up my smartphone and start talking and expect my friend Bob on the other end to listen. I have to dial a phone number for Bob, and then I have to wait for Bob's phone to ring. Once his phone is ringing, Bob can answer that phone, he's going to say hello, Anna here says hello, and once that happens then Anna can say, hey, I need some help. And Bob can say, oh, okay, and they can have that conversation. My point here is that in order for Anna to be able to communicate with Bob, we have to go through that process of dialing the phone, waiting for it to ring, waiting for Bob to say hello, I say hello. Once that happens then I can send any information I want. Transmission Control Protocol does this in data networking. This is also called TCP, and what it does is it sets up a session between our workstation and the server so that we can send data between these two devices. This is the transport layer. The transport layer in networking is responsible for setting up a session typically using TCP. It has a handshake process, and it builds a connection, and it uses the network layer to find where in the world those devices are. It uses the data link layer to communicate those messages from device to device to device to device until they reach their destinations, and that all happens on the physical layer, which is our wires and cables that connect our network together. Next, we need a way to transfer information that's in a usable format. One of those ways is to use a web browser and browse to a website like Google.com and then retrieve a web page. The website is nothing more than a document with information in it. The web browser is an application that makes use of a protocol in order to request and transfer information. In order to get the website to our workstation, we're going to make a request of the server to say, send us the website. The server's going to respond with a document that is the website, and we're going to use a protocol called Hypertext Transfer Protocol. This is also known as HTTP, and it has a sibling called HTTPS, which is the encrypted version of it. HTTP and HTTPS, they transfer documents that are written in a language called HyperText Markup Language, or HTML. We're using HTTP to transfer HTML documents. Our website is written in some form of HTML, and we use HTTP or HTTPS to transfer those. All of this is happening outside of our process of building a session between our two workstations or identifying the location of those devices with IP addresses or having protocols that allow us to transfer information from our computer to the router to the cable modem and so on. All this is happening at the application layer of the OSI model. The OSI model is seven layers, and you've noticed that I have skipped two of them. The OSI model was written in the 70s when they had different networking needs and other protocols involved. So there's two layers that I have not talked about now, 5 and 6. So what's going on with that? Well, let's talk about it. First, let's talk about the presentation layer. The presentation layer is layer 6, and we don't really use the presentation layer anymore. There's a reason for that. Back in the 70s, there were several types of systems. There were a lot of open source systems that universities used, and then IBM had systems as well, and IBM developed very proprietary protocols that were similar but different than the ones used in university settings. Let's say we have this message of "Hello." Well, in order to create Hello in a language that the computer understands and can encode, when we type on the keyboard, each one of these letters, each of those is mapped to a hexadecimal value. It's a 8-bit hexadecimal value, and it's called ASCII, which stands for American Standard Code for Information Interchange. ASCII is still used today. When we type on our keyboard, it is still translated to these values in ASCII you. So if I translate, Hello to ASCII. In

IBM-land, they used a completely different number system in order to encode each key of the keyboard. Each keystroke that meant Don't Panic got encoded differently. And EBCDIC, which stands for Extended Binary Coded Decimal Interchange Code, is IBM's version. It was their proprietary version. And in order for a system that used ASCII to communicate with a system that used EBCDIC, we needed some layer of the OSI model to translate from one system to the other, and that's what we intended to do with the presentation layer. That has all become quite antiquated, and we really don't do much with this anymore. You may find in textbooks that they're going to say, JPEG and MPEG and whatnot happen at the presentation layer, and that might be the case. But really, those are outside of the OSI model, and we're ultimately going to be using application layer protocols in order to transfer information, and we really don't worry too much about the presentation layer. The session layer is another layer. There are some protocols that do operate at the session layer. However, for networking purposes, we don't stress too much about classifying something as a session layer protocol. Ultimately, we consider it to be part of the application layer. In summary we've introduced the OSI model, we talked about the seven layers of it, we started by modeling that telephone call and thinking about how we had to vibrate the air and the entire process that needed to happen in order to make that phone call, as well as another idea of a protocol where we actually had to dial the phone, wait for it to ring, say hello before we could transfer messages between the two devices. Then we talked pretty in depth about all of the components of the OSI model and how they relate to networking. Remember, the OSI model gives us a very precise order of operations that we can work with. It gives us a space to categorize each protocol so that when we are working with networking, we understand which protocols are involved and why.

# Chapter 4 Encapsulation and the OSI Model

In this chapter, we're going to take a look at encapsulation and the OSI model. We just talked about the OSI model and how each of the layers have a specific purpose and now we're going to go be a little more technical about it and introduce how those layers are being used here to send data. So our goals are to review the OSI model, then to introduce the concept of encapsulation, and then I'm going to describe encapsulation layer by layer of the OSI model. Remember, we're going to not worry about layers 5 and 6, we're just going to stick to the application, transport, network, data link, and physical. And as a reminder, remember the application layer, we're typically dealing with a protocol that allows us to transfer specific types of data in a specific way. Our transport layer is going to set up a session between the two endpoints, between our client and our server. The network layer is going to give us the path that we can take through the internet or through a network to get from our client to our server. The data link layer is going to let us make the individual hops between our client and our switch, the switch and the router, the router and our cable modem, the cable modem and the internet, and so on. The data link layer is going to allow for that. Then the physical layer is going to be where we actually move the bits of information, either as an electromagnetic wave in the case of wireless or as a light signal in the case of fiber optics or as an electrical impulse in the case of a copper wire. So, let's take a look at how this happens. So if we go to Google.com on our workstation, we send that information out onto the internet, and then it transfers the website to our computer, and this all seems to happen magically, seamlessly, and typically very quickly. When we're actually doing this, though, what we're going to do is we're going to take that website, and this is our actual application layer information, in the case of going to a website, we're going to use a protocol called HTTP, or Hypertext Transfer Protocol. Websites are written in a language called HTML, or Hypertext Markup Language, and we use Hypertext Transfer Protocol, HTTP, to transfer it. This application layer protocol, HTTP, is what we're using the transfer it. When we are working with this, these websites tend to be quite large, so we need to be able to break up that website into smaller chunks so we can successfully get it to the client. We're going to find out at the end of this encapsulation process that some protocols, specifically Ethernet, has a maximum amount of data that we can transfer for each frame that we send. For each chunk of data that we send across the network, we have a maximum amount of data that we can send in each one. Once we have this application layer, it's going to work in conjunction with the transport layer to take that data, break it into smaller pieces, and then add it to a header. We're going to put a header on this data at the transport layer. The transport layer, since it's setting up a session between our client and our server, we're going to have specific information in there to allow that to happen. In this case, it's a source port, a destination port number, some flags, which is just some general information about what's happening in the transaction, a sequence number, an acknowledgement number, and those keep track of how much data has been sent and received. This is like if you're sending a birthday card to your dad. You would fill out the birthday card, you put any information in the card that you want, much like our website here for Google.com, there's lots of websites out there and this particular one is Google, so we can take any information we want and we take that card and we put it inside of an envelope and we seal it up, and then we write on the envelope the destination address, which is our dad's name and address, and then we put a return address on it, which is our name and address. We're taking this information, we're putting it inside of an envelope. This particular envelope is the transport layer, and we call this envelope a segment. So any data that we have with a header at the transport layer, we call a segment. This particular segment header, or transport layer header, is a TCP header, and we're going to learn more about TCP later. For now, we just need to know that this information allows the client and the server to set up a session and keep track of what data has been sent and received. That's just one component of this transaction. In order to know where we are sending this data, we need to tell it what the source and destination IP addresses are. We need to know where on the internet or on a network the server and the client are. We take our transport layer information, which is going to keep that session between our endpoints going, and then we send it down to the network layer, so we take our segment and it becomes the payload of our network layer, and then we add the header, we add the source IP, destination IP, a value called the TTL, or time to live, which tells it how far this packet can travel at a maximum distance, as well as some other information that we add into the network layer header to make this transaction work correctly. It's not important at this level of understanding of data networking. Now we have our segment inside of the payload of our network layer header. This is called a packet. So, any time we have some data that we're transferring with a network layer header, this is a packet. So it's a chunk of data with a network layer header. This particular one is an IP header, or Internet Protocol. Specifically, Internet Protocol version 4. And we're going to learn more about IP as we go throughout this book. Our network layer header is going to allow us to know what two endpoints on the internet, or any network, we're going to send this information to. In order to get our packet to go from one device to the next, from our workstation to the switch, from the switch to the router, from the router to the cable modem, from the cable modem out to the internet, and all of the hops that go along the internet, we're going to need a data link layer header, so we send our network layer packet down to the data link layer and we put it in a frame. A frame is just a chunk of data with a data link layer header. In this particular case, this is an Ethernet header, so this is going to be an Ethernet frame, and we'll often use the Ethernet frame when we're sending data from our workstation to the switch, from the switch to our router, from a router to the cable modem. However, once we get to the cable modem, we're going to use a different protocol there which requires a different frame. What we'll end up doing is taking the packet out of the frame and putting it into a new frame, and this happens consistently throughout the transaction as removing the data across the internet. The packet will remain the same; the frame header will change as it goes from segment to segment to segment. In our frame, especially an Ethernet frame, remember earlier I said that there's a maximum amount of data that we can send in that? Here, our data is still intact here, that chunk of website that we're sending is still encapsulated inside of this frame. There's also a transport layer header, there's a network layer header, and then we have this Ethernet header. When we're working with this, especially Ethernet, the data part of this can have something called a maximum transmission unit for Ethernet, or MTU, and for Ethernet that's typically 1500 bytes. We can make that larger in some cases, but in most cases 1500 bytes is the maximum amount of payload, including the packet header, including the segment header that we can send using an Ethernet frame. We have to break up the data into these smaller chunks to allow this to happen. We can make that larger in some cases. Lots of times inside of a data center for specific applications, we will increase that MTU size, but for regular day-to-day use on our networks from our PCs, we rarely adjust that size. Once we have our frame constructed with the source MAC address, destination

MAC address, and then layer 3 protocol that we're using, we can then take that frame, send it down to the physical layer. When we send it down to the physical layer, what's going to happen here is we're going to convert that into 1s and 0s, and then the 1s and 0s are converted into a signal. That signal could be a light signal that we send across fiber optics, it could be an electrical pulse that we send across a copper wire or it might be an electromagnetic signal that we send with wireless. So in order for us to get the website from Google over to our workstation, we have to send all that data up and down the OSI model in order to make all the hops that we need to make in order to get it from our server over to our workstation. That involves taking our application layer information, putting it inside of a segment, taking the segment, putting it inside of a packet, taking the packet, putting it inside of a frame, and then sending it across the wire. In summary, we first reviewed the OSI model. We then introduced this concept of encapsulation, like taking a birthday card and putting it inside of an envelope; however, in this case we're taking that birthday card, putting it in an envelope, pushing that envelope inside of another envelope, putting that envelope inside of another envelope before we put it in the mail. I described the encapsulation concept layer by layer of the OSI model and we introduced the concept of segment at the transport layer, packet at the network layer, and frame at the data link layer. This is literally the foundation of everything else we are going to discuss in data networking.

# Chapter 5 Network Protocols and Port Numbers

In the following chapters, we're going to look at protocols and port numbers for those protocols, and we're specifically looking at application layer protocols. We're going to start with data transfer protocols. Almost everything in data networking is moving data from one device to another; however, there are some that meet this criteria more than others because we're actually moving a file that we're using as users versus doing some kind of network support or other utility. We're also going to look at authentication protocols, we're going to look at network service protocols too, things that help make our network run. We're going to look at network management protocols, stuff that we use as a network engineer to make sure the network is running smoothly. We're going to look at some audiovisual protocols, specifically the things that make our voiceover IP phone work. Then last, we're going to look at database protocols, specifically SQL Database protocols that we use in order to access database information. If we take a look again at our OSI model, we're going to be looking at application layer protocols in this particular module; however, there is a transport layer component that we're also looking at, and that's going to be the port number. You may remember on encapsulation and the OSI model that when we build the segment, we put in a source and destination port number, and this port number is going to be directly related to an application layer protocol. So let's take a look at these application layer protocols, starting with transferring data. Whenever we go on our workstation and we ask for a website like Google.com, we are asking for an HTML document to be transferred from the server to our workstation. In order to do this, we're going to be using one of two protocols, which are effectively the same thing, HTTP or HTTPS. This is hypertext transfer protocol or hypertext transfer protocol secure. These protocols allow us to transfer an HTML document between a server and a client. At the application layer, layer 7, we call them by their names here, HTTP and HTTPS. But at the transport layer, they are associated with a specific port number. In the case of HTTP, it's port 80 and in the case of HTTPS, it is port 443. Port 80 and port 443, we typically associate with using web services. When we're using HTTPS on port 443, you will often hear engineers and people talk about using SSL, secure socket layer, or TLS, transport layer security. TLS and SSL sound very different. However, they are the same thing. You will read documents on the internet that claim that SSL works for function X, and TLS works for function Y. You may hear some fancy stories about how they're different and separate, but the reality is it is literally the same protocol. They just changed the name of it right around 2000. The late '90s, early 2000s, they changed the name from SSL to TLS. This is complicated and beyond the scope of this book. Just remember that SSL and TLS are the same thing, and we use transport layer security to provide the encryption when we're using HTTPS. Not all of the files that we transfer when we're working with a data network are going to be HTML files via a website. Sometimes we have files on our workstation that need to get transferred to a server or to a network device, which means that we'd have some kind of file here that needs to get sent to the server. Or maybe there's some specific files that are not HTML files on a server that we need to access and download to our workstation. So when we're working with file transfer, we have several options. These three options here, FTP, SFTP, and TFTP all kind of rely on the same general technology. These are all called file transfer protocol of some kind. FTP, file transfer protocol. SFTP you can imagine is secure FTP and TFTP, this is a little bit of an odd one here. This is trivial file transfer protocol. FTP operates on two separate port numbers, port 20 and 21. It is somewhat of a messy protocol, especially if we have to use it through a firewall. Secure FTP is FTP with encryption. It operates on port 22, which we're going to find out is the same exact port number for another utility that we use called SSH or Secure Shell. The reason that it's the same port number is that we're actually creating an SSH connection and then using FTP on top of it. But for now, you have to remember that SFTP uses port 22. Then TFTP uses port 69. When we are working with these, TFTP is typically going to be used to transfer small files, and I have used TFTP most in my career to transfer an operating system file from my workstation that I use to manage the data network. Use that to transfer some operating system file or upgrade to a device, like a router or a switch, in order to have the file on that device so I can upgrade the device to the latest operating system. FTP, SFTP, TFTP are all used to transfer files, and they all have generally the same type of operation. There is one more from Microsoft called SMB, which stands for server message block. If you work in a large business and you have a shared network drive mounted on your workstation, typically we're using SMB as the protocol for this. What it allows us to do is mount a drive on our Windows workstation or other workstations. With SMB then, we can actually just browse that drive as if it were a local drive on our workstation, yet it is a network drive. We can copy files from that drive to our workstation or copy files from our workstation up to that drive, and it's going to use server message block to transfer that file instead of these other FTP varieties. The next application layer protocols we're going to take a look at are email. So email is a way of transferring a file from a server to a client again. We're just using a different format this time, and we're using an email format. There are three methods that we're going to need in order to transfer email. We have POP3, we have IMAP, and we have SMTP. POP3 is Post Office Protocol version 3, IMAP is Internet Message Access Protocol, and SMTP is Simple Mail Transfer Protocol. POP3 and IMAP are typically reserved for retrieving mail from a server to the client. And SMTP is used to send mail from a client to the server. So when we're configuring email clients, usually we need to configure either POP or IMAP, as well as SMTP. These protocols are still used today, and they're common. However, the way we configure them has changed pretty drastically over the last 10 years. Mail services like Gmail, Outlook, Yahoo Mail, and others have changed the way we configure our devices for email. A lot of times, we just say that we're using Google, we put in our username and password, and it automatically configures all the protocols for us versus what I may have had to do in 1999. I would have to actually go in and configure all the details of my email system, configuring the correct POP3 server, the correct port number, the correct SMTP server and its correct port number, as well as my credentials. Time has changed on how we configure and use this, but we still need to know that POP3, IMAP, and SMTP are used for email. All three of these have two transport layer port numbers they can use. If you've seen a theme so far here, we've been talking about unencrypted and encrypted transfer of messages. POP3 here for the unencrypted POP3, it's port 110. Encrypted is port 995. For IMAP, we have unencrypted on port 143 and encrypted on port 993. Then for SMTP, we have port 25 for unencrypted and port 465 for encrypted. We typically can't just change the port number in our system to make it encrypted. We have to have that protocol installed and enabled on our devices, which, in most modern mail clients, these protocols are enabled and we can use them.

## Chapter 6 DHCP, DNS & NTP

When we talk about authentication, usually we're talking about authentication of a client to a server. When we're using LDAP, oftentimes we have a workstation, especially in a corporate office, where we have to use a username and password to log into that client. What some authentication services can do is instead of having those credentials stored locally on your workstation, like you might have with your home computer, the credentials are actually stored on a server inside of the organization's data center. That way it doesn't matter what workstation you log onto in the workstation, your settings and desktop and mapped drives and whatnot will all show up the same on your client workstation, regardless of which one you're using. There's two protocols that we use for this. It's Lightweight Directory Access Protocol. One is not encrypted; one is with the S and it's encrypted. We put in a username and password on the client, we send it to the server, and the server will then send a token back saying yes, this user is authenticated. Then after that, the server may send additional information that has user settings and whatnot for the client. For LDAP, we're going to use port 389. For LDAP secure or LDAPs, we're going to use port 636 at the transport layer. Next, we're going to talk about a series of network protocols that we use for network services. The first one is called Dynamic Host Configuration Protocol, or DHCP. DHCP is responsible for giving your workstation an IP address when it first is plugged into the network. IP addresses are and identifier for your device on the network. It's one of the identifiers for your device on the network, and it operates at the network layer. The IP address, it has very specific properties, and it has to meet very specific criteria in order for your client to be able to communicate with the rest of the network or the internet. Instead of having users configure this or configure them manually, we oftentimes will use a DHCP server to do this. As a matter of fact, this is the case in your home network. Your cable modem or your cable modem router or your wireless access point, all those devices have capabilities to offer a DHCP server. That way, when you turn on your device and you connect it to the wireless network or you plug your device into the wired network, it automatically gets an IP address. When we plug the client into the network, we're going to send out a discover message. This DHCP server then is going to reply with something called an offer message. The offer message is going to have the IP address, a subnet mask, the default gateway, DNS server, possibly some other information as well. Then what'll happen is the client will respond back and say, yes, I accept that, and then the server will respond back and say great. I acknowledge that. I've added it to my database. DHCP is going to use port numbers 67 and 68 in order to operate on a network. The next network service we're going to take a look at is probably the most important service on the internet. It is Domain Name System, or Domain Name Service, DNS. This is also called a name server sometimes. DNS allows us to take names like pluralsight.com, google.com, facebook.com, you name your favorite website that you go to often, and it allows us to translate the name google.com into an IP address that we can actually use to transfer information at the network layer. The network layer of the OSI model uses IP addresses as a source and a destination of the packet so that we can move that packet, usually containing a segment of information and maybe some other application layer data, we can use that packet then to move from our client to the device that we're trying to reach without having to know the specific IP address of every device that we're trying to reach on the internet. The way this works is when I go to google.com on my workstation, I will first send a message to the DNS server saying, what is the IP address of google.com? The DNS server will reply to me with the IP address of google.com. Then, after I have that information, I can construct my packet using the source IP address of my client and the destination IP address of google.com. Here I'm saying 216.58.216.205, which is google.com, send the website that you have available to 203.0.113.68, which is my client workstation. We send that to the internet over to Google, and then Google can send back the website to my workstation. So DNS, what it's doing for us is it's resolving names that we know as individual people because it's easy to remember something like Google or Facebook. It's much easier to remember that than it is to remember these series of four digit numbers between 0 and 255. It's going to be nearly impossible to remember, plus those IP addresses oftentimes change depending upon where you are in the world. DNS is super critical, and we have found that it's an easy place for attackers to attack a DNS server and really mess up how we resolve names into IP addresses and can cause some real serious issues. We have to take some extra security when we're setting up DNS servers to make sure that they don't get compromised by nefarious agents trying to attack our networks. DNS works on port 53. Whenever we see DNS over port 53, we'll know that that DNS is not actually encrypted. There is a newer version of DNS coming out. It's actually not a new version of DNS. It's a new version of transporting DNS information where we actually do it over HTTPS, so it's called DNS over HTTPS, or DoH, and that's going to use the same port number that HTTPS uses, which is 443. We don't need to know that so much for the Net+ certification exam, but know that in the next several years we should start to see DNS start to operate over HTTPS, making it more secure because it will be encrypted. The next network service that is incredibly critical on our network is Network Time Protocol. Network time Protocol is it's a device on the network that has a clock on it. That clock is usually synchronized with some government-run atomic clock, so it has a very precise time. Our server on the network would go retrieve the precise time from some atomic clock someplace out on the internet and then synchronize it locally so that when local clients need to know how to set their clocks, they can send a message to our NTP server, and the NTP server will reply back with the time. In this case, it's 3:00 pm, and now the client can set its time. This will include the date on the workstation. NTP is important because services like encryption will oftentimes validate whether or not a server that we're connecting to is valid by checking a certificate, and the certificate is often only valid for a specific period of time, so we need some type of clock to validate that the time of the certificate is okay to use. Also, we have log messages that are stored on clients, servers, network devices, firewalls,etc., and those logs need a precise time so that if an event occurs, whether it be a technical event or a security event, we know exactly the right time that it's happening so we can coordinate that with other device logs on our network. When we use NTP, it uses something called Coordinated Universal Time, or UTC. This is how we accommodate different time zones. The way UTC is set up is if we look at a map of Earth and we zoom into England area, there is an imaginary line called the prime meridian, which runs through Greenwich, England. Greenwich, England is just a little bit east of London, and there's a lot of big events that happened in Greenwich, England. As a matter of fact, at one point in time it was home to the British Navy. The British Navy invented a lot of utilities so that they could travel around the world. The prime meridian is used as our 0 point when calculating UTC. When it is midnight in Greenwich, England, the time is 00:00 UTC. If we zoom out and we take a look at maybe what the time might be in Chicago when it is UTC 00:00, it is -6 hours in Chicago. This is assuming that we're not using daylight savings or that we're at a time when daylight savings is not in effect. I'm ignoring daylight savings here to keep this a little bit more efficient. Know that Network Time Protocol servers do have all of the calculations needed for daylight savings time as well. But to keep this simpler for the moment, we're going to assume no daylight savings time. So if it is at midnight 00:00 UTC in Greenwich, England, it is 6 hours before that in Chicago, or 6 pm. If we look at that same in Utah, at midnight in Greenwich, England, in Utah, it would be 5 pm, 7 hours before that. If we look at another place on Earth here and take a look at the time in New Delhi, New Delhi is +5:30 from UTC, which means that if it is midnight in Greenwich, England, it is 5 hours 30 minutes ahead of that in New Delhi, which is a little bit odd that there's that 30 minutes in there, but it doesn't really matter. It's just a way of measuring what time it is so that we always have the same time no matter where we are on Earth using UTC. So if it's at midnight in Greenwich, England, it is 5:30 in the morning in New Delhi. NTP is a critical service on our network. It uses port 389 when we're talking from the client to the server.

## Chapter 7 SQL Database Protocols

Network management means that oftentimes we have devices on our network that we are going to manage from some central location. This is a way to actually use a command-line interface to access devices around the network, whether it be a server, like a Linux server. Could also be a router, or a switch, or a firewall, or a multitude of other devices that we can access with this. On our Network Administration Workstation, we might SSH to a router, or a switch, or a server, or even a firewall. The devices that we are SSHing to are going to be the server. The device we're SSHing from becomes our client. The next utility we're going to look at is SNMP, or Simple Network Management Protocol. It's a way for devices to send information back to a centralized server, information like log messages, or information about port up and down, or maybe some other event on our device that we configure to tell our SNMP server about. In this case, all the devices that are sending messages to the SNMP server become our client. This could be a server. This could be a router, a switch, a firewall. All these devices can report in to the server what's happening with them, or the server can send out a message to all these devices and say, tell me all the information that you have about your devices that has an SNMP number assigned to it. Those numbers are called MIBs, or management information base, and they can send all that information back to the server then, and the server can use that information to populate a table of all the events that are happening on the devices. Another thing that can happen is if an event happens on a device, like some event happens on that switch that needs attention, what can happen here is we can have an SNMP trap. What that means is that when an event occurs on a device, both good or bad, it can send a message to the SNMP server saying, hey, this event happened. We can configure that central server to send out alerts to the network administrator saying, the network is on fire; we better fix it. SNMP uses ports 161 and 162. Another network utility we can use that's very similar to SNMP is syslog. Syslog is a mechanism to take the logs on each one of our devices and send them to a centralized syslog server so they can be correlated with other events on our network. For example, I plug a network device into my switch, that's going to generate an event. The event doesn't have to be anything significant. In this case, it's just that the port changed state from down to up. When that happens with syslog enabled and configured correctly, we will send that syslog message from the client over to the syslog server where it can be recorded, so now the syslog server knows of that event as well. Syslog is going to use port number 514. Another utility we can use here is Remote Desktop Protocol, or RDP. Remote Desktop Protocol allows us to access the graphical user interface of devices on our network when we are not local. We may, on our client, need to configure a Windows Server, so we can use RDP, or Remote Desktop Protocol, to actually make a connection to the server, and then we'll get a screenshot of the graphical user interface of the server that we can then interact with. This operates on port 3389. Let's now talk about some audiovisual protocols now. The audiovisual protocols that we're using allow us to either have Voice over IP phone calls or video phone calls between two organizations. Here we're going to use a protocol called H.323. This operates on port 1720, and that allows for video and audio communication between two devices. Another one we can use here for Voice over IP telephones is SIP, or Session Initiation Protocol. Session Initiation Protocol uses port 5060 and 5061, and it's the protocol we use to transfer voice when we're using our Voice over IP phone to a voice gateway, which gets us out to the rest of the telephone system so we can make calls. Databases themselves also use port numbers. SQL is a protocol called Structured Query Language, and it actually means several things. It can mean the server, like a SQL Server. It can mean the language that we use to access data on that server. It can also be the protocol used to communicate across the network to access that database. There are three flavors of this that are important. We have MySQL, which is open source; we have SQLNet, which is by Oracle; and we have SQL Server, which is a Microsoft product. MySQL operates on port 3306, SQLNet operates on 1521, and SQL Server operates on port 1433. That's a lot of protocols to go over. Some of these protocols we're going to do an even deeper dive later on so that we can best understand how they work. But to wrap up this one, this was really to identify that there's lots of application layer protocols we use to transfer data, and they have an associated port number at the transport layer. These application layer protocols we looked at were data transfer protocols like FTP, SFTP, TFTP, and SMB. We looked at authentication protocols like LDAP. We looked at network service protocols like DHCP, DNS, NTP. We looked at network management protocols like SNMP, SSH. We also looked at some audiovisual protocols like H.323 and SIP, and then also database protocols, specifically for SQL, whether we're using MySQL, SQLNet, or SQL Server. These protocols are the beginnings of what's going to become a much richer and complex but organized compilation that makes data networking work. Next we will go down to the transport layer and take a look at how TCP and UDP work because all of these application layer protocols are either going to use TCP or they're going to use UDP, and there's going to be that specific port number associated with it

In this chapter, we're going to talk about TCP and UDP. Our goals are to talk about transport layer protocols. We've spent a lot of time talking about application layer protocols and their transport layer port number. Now we're going to talk about two transport layer protocols, TCP and UDP, Transmission Control Protocol and User Datagram Protocol and we're going to wrap up by covering some protocol hierarchy so we can see how all of these protocols interact with each other using the guidelines of the OSI model.

| | |
|---|---|
| 7 | Application Layer |
| 6 | Presentation Layer |
| 5 | Session Layer |
| 4 | Transport Layer |
| 3 | Network Layer |
| 2 | Data Link Layer |
| 1 | Physical Layer |

Here's our OSI model again, application, presentation, session, transport, network, data link, and physical. We are going to focus this time on transport layer. The transport layer is responsible for building a session and maintaining a session between two endpoints, typically a client and a server on a data network. Transmission Control Protocol is one of the most popular Layer 4 protocols that we use. Transmission Control Protocol is also called TCP. The way I like to think about TCP is that it is a protocol that initiates communication between two devices. This is a lot like the way we initiate a phone call between ourselves and our friend. Anna wants to make a phone call to her friend, Bob, but in order to do that, she just can't pick up her smartphone and start talking into it and expect Bob to be there. She has to go through a very precise set of steps to reach Bob. So she has to pick up her cell phone and wake it up. She's going to then open up the app for the phone and dial a phone number or find a contact for him, and that's going to cause Bob's phone to ring. Once Bob sees his phone ringing, he can pick up his phone, hit the button to answer it, and then each one of them are going to say a message. And he's going to say, hello, and Anna is going to respond with hello. Now we have established a session for these two individuals to have a conversation with each other. Before that, they could not have a conversation. They were not in the same room. What they needed to do is Anna needed to go through those very precise set of steps, wait for Bob to say hello, she says hello, and now they can transfer any information they want. Built into this conversation are cues and messages that allow each other to understand that the message that was sent was the one received. Anna may say, Bob, I need some help, and Bob may respond and say, I see. Bob may say, wow, that sounds really difficult, and Anna responds with uh-huh. So we send these cues throughout our conversation to validate that the message that was sent was actually received. However, we can also have messages that indicate that we did not receive the message. Anna may say hey, I need some help, and Bob may say, hey, you're breaking up. I can't hear you. Or Bob may say something and later responds with, I don't understand. These are signals that we need to retransmit the information being sent. Then when we're done with the conversation, unless it's some kind of argument where we just hang up the phone, typically we're going to say goodbye to each other. So Anna may say, okay, great, thanks. I'll see you soon for your help. She says goodbye, Bob says goodbye, and then the conversation is over. We don't need those goodbyes to end the conversation. It just makes it more polite. In TCP, we have something called the three-way handshake, and this is a very precise setup process that the client and the server need to go through before we can send information. If I'm trying to receive a website from the web server, before I can do that, I have to go through this TCP process where I first send a message to the web server called a SYN message. The SYN message is the first message to the web server indicating that the client wants to start a conversation. Then what'll happen is the web server will reply with a message called a SYN-ACK. The SYN-ACK is just alerting the client that yes, I'm available for this conversation. Let's get started. And before they get started actually transferring the website though, the client is going to respond with an ACK, or an acknowledgment. So the three-way handshake goes SYN, SYN-ACK, ACK. Once that process is done, now the PC can say, hey, web server, send me that website, and then the web server can reply with a message containing the website. Here's the website, and now it's loaded on the client's computer. When the conversation is all done and the website has finished transferring, the web server or the client will send a message called a FIN, and then the client will respond with a FIN-ACK. Once the FIN-ACK has been sent, the client will respond with its own FIN message, and then the web server is going to reply back to that with a FIN-ACK. So the four-way disconnect is FIN, FIN-ACK, FIN, FIN-ACK. Then the two ends know now that the conversation is over, and now we can no longer send messages between these two devices. Much in the same way that Anna and Bob said goodbye to each other and hung up the phone, now they cannot communicate anymore unless one of them picks up the phone again and dials the phone number, waits for it to ring, answers the phone, then they can send the message again. Same thing is true in TCP. In order for this client and this server to communicate in the future, they will need to send another three-way handshake. That's not the only way to end a conversation in TCP. There's another way here that we call a TCP reset. The TCP reset can be sent from either the web server, and when the TCP reset happens, the conversation is over. It's like Bob or Anna just hanging up the phone and stopping the conversation, right? In order to start that conversation up again, Anna or Bob would have to redial the phone to start that conversation. TCP reset doesn't have to come from the web server; it can also come from the client. The client can just say nope, we're done. Another possibility here is that there's some device in the middle, like a firewall, that's paying attention to this conversation, watching for nefarious activity, and that can actually send a reset as well. However, that is a more sophisticated application of this reset. Regardless, we have several ways to disconnect our conversation. We can either do the four-way disconnect or we can do a reset. Next, let's talk about User Datagram Protocol. UDP works similarly to TCP in that we're going to set up a session between the two devices. However, this time, we're just going to start talking. We're just going to tell the server, hey, send me some data. Then the server, if it receives it and it's able to, it will send the data to the client. And there's no mechanism to make sure that the data sent was actually received. There's no three-way handshake. There's no four-way disconnect. There's no resets. This just works. With UDP, it's no three-way handshake, no reliable communication, no sequence numbers, acknowledgement numbers, and it's used as an efficient way to transfer data. However, we don't use this as much as you think we would because there's no way to validate that the data sent was actually received. Let's now talk about transport layer addressing. We've already talked about port numbers. We've talked about the application layer protocols and their associated transport layer port numbers, so let's take a little bit deeper dive into this. There are two sets of port numbers here. There are server port numbers, which are called well-known and registered port numbers. There are also client port numbers, and these are called ephemeral port numbers. Ephemeral is another word for temporary. When we are working with well-known port numbers, they are typically from 0 to 1023, and then the registered port numbers are from 1024 through 49,151. The ephemeral port number ranges are from 49,152 all the way up to the last port number, 65,535. How does this work? Well-known port numbers are typically port numbers for applications that we have already discussed, HTTP on port 80, HTTPs on port 443, FTP on ports 20 and 21, SSH 22, Telnet on 23. Registered port numbers are going to be for custom applications, and they can both be official and unofficial. There are many games that would use a registered port number. There are other applications that might use a registered port number for like file sharing, a lot of custom software from manufacturers like Dell or Microsoft or IBM, and they come up with a special network application that will use a registered port number. The ephemeral port numbers are going to be used by the client or the PC side of this in order to identify the session that they're creating. If I'm going to send a message to my router, my router is going to act as the server for Telnet. If I'm going to Telnet to my router, what I would do is the source port would be an ephemeral port number. That's my Layer 4 address for my PC. It's going to be source port of let's say 49,152, and the destination port for that would be 23 because I want to reach the Telnet service on my router. All of these protocols that we've been talking about have application layer protocol dependencies.

| HTTP | HTTPs | FTP | SFTP | SMB | POP3 | IMAP | SMTP | LDAPs | LDAP | TFTP |
|------|-------|-----|------|-----|------|------|------|-------|------|------|
| 80 | 443 | 20,21 | 22 | 445 | 110/995 | 143/993 | 25/587 | 636 | 389 | 69 |
| TCP | | | | | | | | | TCP/UDP | UDP |
| IP | | | | | | | | | | |

What this means is that for these protocols that I've listed here, these are all protocols we've talked about before, HTTP, HTTPS, FTP, SFTP, SMB, POP3, IMAP, all of these have a port number that they're assigned to, and we've discussed this, and then in addition to that, they will use a specific transport layer protocol. They will either use TCP, UDP, or they have a possibility of using one or the other. They won't use both at the same time, but they would use one or the other. In this case, most of the popular application layer protocols, including HTTP and HTTPS, our email protocols, our File Transfer Protocols, these are using TCP. LDAP and TFTP can use UDP. As a matter of fact, TFTP only uses UDP to work. All of these protocols will use IP at the network layer. We have application layer of the protocols, we have transport layer port numbers and the associated protocol they're using, and then the network layer protocol for everything is going to be IP. Here are some additional protocol dependencies: Telnet, SSH, and Remote Desktop all use TCP, DNS, SIP, and H.323, SNMP all can use either TCP or UDP. DHCP and NTP, our time protocol there, will use UDP. And all of these protocols will use IP at the network layer.

| Telnet | SSH | RDP | DNS | SIP | H.323 | SNMP | DHCP | NTP |
|--------|-----|-----|-----|-----|-------|------|-------|-----|
| 23 | 22 | 3389 | 53 | 5060 | 1719 | 161 | 68, 69 | 123 |
| TCP | | | TCP/ UDP | | | | UDP | |
| IP | | | | | | | | |

This is a really good introduction to understanding the protocol hierarchy. We have the application layer protocol, which calls a transport layer port number and transport layer protocol, either TCP or UDP, and then below that at the network layer we have Internet Protocol as the network layer protocol we're going to use. In summary we talked about transport layer protocols, both TCP and UDP. We saw TCP was connection-oriented and that we need the three-way handshake in order to build that conversation and a four-way disconnect or a reset to end it. And during the conversation, we have mechanisms to make sure that all the data sent was actually received. UDP, User Datagram Protocol, was a lightweight version of that. No three-way handshake needed. No disconnect needed. We just start sending data. Then last, we looked at that protocol hierarchy and saw the application layer protocols. We talked about the port numbers, the transport layer protocol being used, and then the network layer protocol being used.

## Chapter 9 Binary and Hexadecimal Numbers

In order to really understand what we're going to do next with IP addressing, we need to understand how binary works and how hexadecimal works and how to convert between binary, hexadecimal, and decimal. Our goals are going to be first, introduce the need for binary, review some primary school mathematics so we understand how to count so we can learn how to count in binary then. Then we're going to convert binary to decimal, we're going to convert decimal to binary, and then we're going to introduce hexadecimal and see how we can convert between the three different number formats. To understand binary and give some context, let's start by talking briefly about base 10. We learned this at a very young age; we learned how to count. We count 1 to 9, and then after 9, we add another placeholder and count to 10. That's likely because we have 10 fingers on our hands, and it's likely a very ancient method of counting. However, when we talk about binary, really we're talking about only two placeholders we can have. The position can either be on or it can be off. It can be a 1 or a 0. So when we count in binary, it's going to count a little bit differently with the same rules. It's just a matter of understanding how to apply those rules correctly. Let's do an example here first and count in decimal, or powers of 10, or base 10. All these mean the same exact thing. So when we count in decimal, we count starting with 0 over in the ones placeholder, and we count to 1, 2, 3, 4, 5, 6, 7, 8, 9, and then once we get to 9, we have used up all 10 values 0 through 9 when we're counting. Once we reach that highest level, 9, we need to add a placeholder, and that's the tens placeholder. So then we start counting over again, and now we start with 1 0, or 10, and then we count to 11, 12, 13, leaving our tens placeholder the same in every case and incrementing our ones placeholder until we get all the way up to 99. We'll count 11, 12, 13, 14, 15, 16, 17, 18, 19, and then we increment our tens placeholder to 20. That goes all the way up into the 90s until we reach 99, and then we've maxed out the placeholders for both the tens and the ones, and the number that comes after 99 is 100. Then we count all the way up to 999, and the number after that is 1000, so we add another placeholder. We keep adding these placeholders until we reach the number that we need?

| Ten Millions Place | Millions Place | | Hundred Thousands Place | Ten Thousands Place | Thousands Place | | Hundreds Place | Tens Place | Ones Place |
|---|---|---|---|---|---|---|---|---|---|
| 0 | 0 | , | 1 | 0 | 0 | , | 0 | 0 | 0 |
| 0 | 1 | , | 0 | 0 | 0 | , | 0 | 0 | 0 |
| 1 | 0 | , | 0 | 0 | 0 | , | 0 | 0 | 0 |

We can add more and more and more placeholders here in the decimal system until we reach the number that is important. When we're thinking about decimal, we're thinking about counting in powers of 10, 0 through 9. Computers need to think in binary. All of their circuitry is designed to think either as on or off. Most of the components in computers work with bits, and bits are nothing more than a placeholder for a 1 or a 0. When we're counting in binary, it's going to work just like we counted in decimal; however, we only have two values per placeholder. It's either going to be 0 or the next one is 1. When we count 0 in the 1s placeholder in binary, the next value that we can put there is 1. Once we hit 1, we're out of values to put in the placeholders now, so we have to add a placeholder, and that's when we add the 2s placeholder. Now when we count higher than 1, we're going to count to 1 0. So 1 0 is the third value in binary. It goes 0, 1, 1 0, and then the next placeholder, we're just going to keep the 2s placeholder as a 1 and increment the 1s placeholder by one value, which becomes 1 1. That's not 11. This is 1 1. It actually equates to 3. And we're going to look at how to get that conversion to work in just a little bit, but for now, we're just going to be counting here in binary. You should be able to see now once we reach 1 1, all the values that we can increment in the 2s placeholder have been used up, 0 and 1, all the placeholders in the 1s placeholder have been used up, again, 0 and 1, so we need to add another placeholder, and it's going to be the 4s placeholder. So after 1 1 in binary comes 1 0 0. Next, we're going to increment the 1s placeholder by one value to bring into 1 0 1, then 1 1 0, then 1 1 1. You might see a pattern forming here with binary.

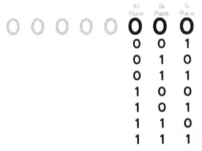

| | | | | 4s Place | 2s Place | 1s Place |
|---|---|---|---|---|---|---|
| O | O | O | O | O | **O** | **O** | **O** |
| | | | | 0 | 0 | 1 |
| | | | | 0 | 1 | 0 |
| | | | | 0 | 1 | 1 |
| | | | | 1 | 0 | 0 |
| | | | | 1 | 0 | 1 |
| | | | | 1 | 1 | 0 |
| | | | | 1 | 1 | 1 |

My brain seems to be tuned into patterns pretty well, and one of the things we can see here is that if we look in the 1s placeholder column and we ignore the rest, we see that the 1s placeholder, as we're counting, goes 0 1 0 1 0 1 as we go down that column. If we look at the 2s placeholder, it goes 0 0 1 1 0 0 1 1 as we count down the column. If we look in the 4s placeholder, it goes 0 0 0 0 1 1 1 1. So as we're counting through these, there's going to be a pattern forming here that we should pay attention to. If the pattern doesn't make sense to you right now, that's okay. Don't worry about it. We're just going to continue to follow the rules here. In our last value here, we've used up 1 1 1 in all of our placeholders. It means we need to add another placeholder, and in this case, it's going to be the 8s placeholder.

| | | | 8s Place | 4s Place | 2s Place | 1s Place |
|---|---|---|---|---|---|---|
| O | O | O | O | **O** | **O** | **O** | **O** |
| | | | 0 | 0 | 0 | 1 |
| | | | 0 | 0 | 1 | 0 |
| | | | 0 | 0 | 1 | 1 |
| | | | 0 | 1 | 0 | 0 |
| | | | 0 | 1 | 0 | 1 |
| | | | 0 | 1 | 1 | 0 |
| | | | 0 | 1 | 1 | 1 |

So in the 8s placeholder then, all I've done is add 0s in the 8s placeholder then. Next, we're going to scroll up here and start counting again because now we've used up 1 1 1 in the 4s, 2s, and 1s. Now we're going to put 1 in the 8s placeholder and start counting all over again, 1 0 0 1, 1 0 1 0, 1 0 1 1, 1 1 0 0, 1 1 0 1, 1 1 1 0, and 1 1 1 1.

| | | | | 8s Place | 4s Place | 2s Place | 1s Place |
|---|---|---|---|---|---|---|---|
| 0 | 0 | 0 | 0 | 1 | 0 | 0 | 0 |
| | | | | 1 | 0 | 0 | 1 |
| | | | | 1 | 0 | 1 | 0 |
| | | | | 1 | 0 | 1 | 1 |
| | | | | 1 | 1 | 0 | 0 |
| | | | | 1 | 1 | 0 | 1 |
| | | | | 1 | 1 | 1 | 0 |
| | | | | 1 | 1 | 1 | 1 |

Now that there is a 1 in each of the placeholders, we can't have any more values here, we've maxed it out, we're going to add another placeholder. It's going to be the 16s placeholder. Then once we get to the maximum value there, we add another one, the 32s placeholder, then the 64s, then the 128s. If we keep counting, we'll go 256, then 512, then 1024, then 2048, and so on. So every placeholder is going to be double the previous placeholder. That brings us now to converting from binary to decimal. We saw how we count in binary. Now let's see if we can do some conversion. Converting from binary to decimal is actually pretty easy. These 1s and 0s are literally just on/off switches, and what we do is we multiply the value of the placeholder times the placeholder itself.

In this case with 11000000, what we do is we start at the 128s and we say okay, there's a 1 in the 128s, so 128 times 1, and then we say there's a 1 in the 64s, so 1 times 64, then 32 is 0 times 32 all the way down to 1. So we have 128, plus 64, plus 0, plus 0, plus 0, plus 0, plus 0, plus 0, and we end up with 192.

In binary, 11000000 equals 192. If we try a different number of 00010110, we're going to apply this same format here again, 0 times 128 is 0, 0 times 64 is 0, 0 times 32 is 0, 1 times 16 is 16, 0 times 8 is 0, 1 times 4 is 4, 1 times 2 is 2, and 1 times 0 is 0, we add those all up and we get 22.

So 10110 is 22. Let's try a few more. This one, as a series of ons and offs. If the value of the placeholder is 0, it's off, we don't count it. If it's a 1, it's on, we do count it. Here we have 0, plus 64, plus 0, plus 0, plus 0, plus 4, plus 2, plus 0, we end up with 70.

=70

Let's try a different one of, 11001000, on, on, off, off, on, off, off, off. We get 128, plus 64, plus 0, plus 8, plus 0, plus 0, plus 0, that equals 200.

=200

## Chapter 10 How to Convert Decimal to Binary

Now that we've seen how to convert from binary to decimal, it's a pretty easy process, converting from decimal into binary is a little bit more complex, it has to ask a few more questions in order to get this to work out. If we have the value of 210 here in decimal and we want to convert this to binary, we have to start by asking some questions. The question goes like this, can I subtract 128 from the number 210 and end up with a positive number or 0? And the answer here is yes we can, and if the answer is yes, then we subtract 128 from our value of 210, that leaves 82. 128, that placeholder is going to be an on because we put a yes there. We'll come back to that.

| 128s<br>Place | 64s<br>Place | 32s<br>Place | 16s<br>Place | 8s<br>Place | 4s<br>Place | 2s<br>Place | 1s<br>Place |
|---|---|---|---|---|---|---|---|
| Can we<br>subtract **128**<br>from **210**? | Can we<br>subtract **64**<br>from **82**? | | | | | | |
| YES<br>**210**<br>**-128**<br>= **82** | | | | | | | |

So let me go to the 64's placeholder and we use the number that we calculated in 128 and can we subtract 64 from 82 and end up with a positive number or 0? And the answer is yes, we can. So 82 minus 64 leaves 18.

| 128s Place | 64s Place | 32s Place | 16s Place | 8s Place | 4s Place | 2s Place | 1s Place |
|---|---|---|---|---|---|---|---|
| Can we subtract **128** from 210? | Can we subtract **64** from 82? | Can we subtract **32** from 18? | | | | | |
| YES | YES | | | | | | |
| 210 | 82 | | | | | | |
| -128 | -64 | | | | | | |
| = 82 | = 18 | | | | | | |

Can we subtract 32 from 18 and end up with a positive number? And the answer is no, we can't. If we subtract 32 from 18, we're going to end up with a negative number so we can't do that transaction.

| 128s Place | 64s Place | 32s Place | 16s Place | 8s Place | 4s Place | 2s Place | 1s Place |
|---|---|---|---|---|---|---|---|
| Can we subtract **128** from 210? | Can we subtract **64** from 82? | Can we subtract **32** from 18? | Can we subtract **16** from 18? | | | | |
| YES | YES | NO | | | | | |
| 210 | 82 | | | | | | |
| -128 | -64 | | | | | | |
| = 82 | = 18 | | | | | | |

How about 16? Can we subtract 16 from 18? The answer is yes, we can. We are left with 2, 18 minus 16 is 2, that's a positive number or 0.

| 128s Place | 64s Place | 32s Place | 16s Place | 8s Place | 4s Place | 2s Place | 1s Place |
|---|---|---|---|---|---|---|---|
| Can we subtract **128** from 210? | Can we subtract **64** from 82? | Can we subtract **32** from 18? | Can we subtract **16** from 18? | | | | |
| YES | YES | NO | YES | | | | |
| 210 | 82 | | 18 | | | | |
| -128 | -64 | | -16 | | | | |
| = 82 | = 18 | | = 2 | | | | |

How about eight? Can we subtract eight from two. Nope, it's going to end up with a negative number.

| 128s Place | 64s Place | 32s Place | 16s Place | 8s Place | 4s Place | 2s Place | 1s Place |
|---|---|---|---|---|---|---|---|
| Can we subtract **128** from **210**? | Can we subtract **64** from **82**? | Can we subtract **32** from **18**? | Can we subtract **16** from **18**? | Can we subtract **8** from **2**? | Can we subtract **4** from **2**? | | |
| YES | YES | NO | YES | NO | | | |
| 210 | 82 | | 18 | | | | |
| -128 | -64 | | -16 | | | | |
| = 82 | = 18 | | = 2 | | | | |

How about four? Can we subtract four from two? Nope, that would end up with a -2.

| 128s Place | 64s Place | 32s Place | 16s Place | 8s Place | 4s Place | 2s Place | 1s Place |
|---|---|---|---|---|---|---|---|
| Can we subtract **128** from **210**? | Can we subtract **64** from **82**? | Can we subtract **32** from **18**? | Can we subtract **16** from **18**? | Can we subtract **8** from **2**? | Can we subtract **4** from **2**? | Can we subtract **2** from **2**? | |
| YES | YES | NO | YES | NO | NO | | |
| 210 | 82 | | 18 | | | | |
| -128 | -64 | | -16 | | | | |
| = 82 | = 18 | | = 2 | | | | |

Can we subtract 2 from 2 and end up with a positive number or 0? The answer is yes, we end up with 0.

| 128s Place | 64s Place | 32s Place | 16s Place | 8s Place | 4s Place | 2s Place | 1s Place |
|---|---|---|---|---|---|---|---|
| Can we subtract **128** from **210**? | Can we subtract **64** from **82**? | Can we subtract **32** from **18**? | Can we subtract **16** from **18**? | Can we subtract **8** from **2**? | Can we subtract **4** from **2**? | Can we subtract **2** from **2**? | Can we subtract **1** from **0**? |
| YES | YES | NO | YES | NO | NO | YES | |
| 210 | 82 | | 18 | | | 2 | |
| -128 | -64 | | -16 | | | -2 | |
| = 82 | = 18 | | = 2 | | | = 0 | |

Can we subtract 1 from 0 and end up with a positive number or 0? No we can't that, would be -1 so we put no there.

| 128s Place | 64s Place | 32s Place | 16s Place | 8s Place | 4s Place | 2s Place | 1s Place |
|---|---|---|---|---|---|---|---|
| Can we subtract 128 from 210? | Can we subtract 64 from 82? | Can we subtract 32 from 18? | Can we subtract 16 from 18? | Can we subtract 8 from 2? | Can we subtract 4 from 2? | Can we subtract 2 from 2? | Can we subtract 1 from 0? |
| YES | YES | NO | YES | NO | NO | YES | NO |
| 210 -128 = 82 | 82 -64 = 18 | | 18 -16 = 2 | | | 2 -2 = 0 | |

In order to convert this, we're going through this iterative process and saying, can I subtract this value? How about this one? And every time we say get a yes, we do the calculation and we end up with a new value. So here, wherever there is a yes, we put a 1, wherever there is a no, we put a 0 and this is our binary number. So 210 in binary is 11010010.

| 128s Place | 64s Place | 32s Place | 16s Place | 8s Place | 4s Place | 2s Place | 1s Place |
|---|---|---|---|---|---|---|---|
| **1** | **1** | **0** | **1** | **0** | **0** | **1** | **0** |
| YES | YES | NO | YES | NO | NO | YES | NO |

Let's do a different number of 47.

# 47

| 128s Place | 64s Place | 32s Place | 16s Place | 8s Place | 4s Place | 2s Place | 1s Place |
|---|---|---|---|---|---|---|---|
| Can we subtract 128 from 47? | Can we subtract 64 from 47? | Can we subtract 32 from 47? | Can we subtract 16 from 15? | Can we subtract 8 from 15? | Can we subtract 4 from 7? | Can we subtract 2 from 3? | Can we subtract 1 from 1? |
| NO | NO | YES | NO | YES | YES | YES | YES |
| | | 47 -32 = 15 | | 15 -8 = 7 | 7 -4 = 3 | 3 -2 = 1 | 1 -1 = 0 |

So can we subtract 128 from 47? No. How about 64? Can we subtract 64 from 47? Nope. Thirty-two, can we subtract 32 from 47? Yes, yes we can and that leaves us with 15. So how about this? Can we subtract 16 from 15. Nope, that would leave us with -1. How about eight? The answer is yes. It's going to leave us with seven. How about four? The answer is yes, it's going to leave us with three. How about two? The answer is yes, we can leave, we can subtract two from three, that leaves one. Can subtract 1 from 1 and end up with 0? Yes we can. So for 47 now, we end up with 00101111.

| 128s Place | 64s Place | 32s Place | 16s Place | 8s Place | 4s Place | 2s Place | 1s Place |
|:---:|:---:|:---:|:---:|:---:|:---:|:---:|:---:|
| **0** | **0** | **1** | **0** | **1** | **1** | **1** | **1** |
| NO | NO | YES | NO | YES | YES | YES | YES |

Whenever we're describing a binary number, if we're always describing an 8-bit binary number, it's completely okay to lead with the zeros in the beginning of the number. However, generally speaking, it's not necessary. We can ignore zeros that are in the higher placeholders. In this case, if I wanted to say 47 in binary, I could just say 101111. In the same way I could add a bunch of zeros in front of the 47 and say at 000047 in decimal and that's still going to equal 47. So we can either, in binary, we can either say those leading zeros in our binary number or we can ignore them. Hexadecimal requires us to be able to convert from binary to decimal, and then once we convert from binary to decimal, this will start to be easier to see how easy it is to convert to hexadecimal because each hexadecimal value is represented by four binary bits. If we start counting, the counting is going to be real easy in the beginning. So on the left-hand column there, I'm going to count up in 4 bits of binary from 0 to 8.

## Hexadecimal

| Binary | Decimal | | Hexadecimal |
|--------|---------|---|-------------|
| 0000 | 0 | 0 | |
| 0001 | 1 | 1 | |
| 0010 | 2 | 2 | |
| 0011 | 3 | 3 | |
| 0100 | 4 | 4 | |
| 0101 | 5 | 5 | |
| 0110 | 6 | 6 | |
| 0111 | 7 | 7 | |
| 1000 | 8 | 8 | |

## Hexadecimal

| Binary | Decimal | | Hexadecimal |
|--------|---------|---|-------------|
| 1001 | 9 | 9 | |
| 1010 | 10 | A | |
| 1011 | 11 | B | |
| 1100 | 12 | C | |
| 1101 | 13 | D | |
| 1110 | 14 | E | |
| 1111 | 15 | F | |
| 10000 | 16 | 10 | |

So 0000 in binary is 0 in decimal, 0 in hexadecimal. 0001 in binary is 1, 0010 is 2, 0011 is 3, 0100 is 4, 0101 is 5, 0110 is 6, 0111 is 7, 1000 is 8, 1001 is 9, and then 1010 in binary is 10 in decimal. It's the 8s place holder, plus the 2s placeholder. In binary, that's 10. In hexadecimal, instead of coming up with a new number symbol, which we don't really have, instead, we're going to use a capital letter A. So if you remember back to the time where we were looking at an IP address, specifically an IP version 6 address, it had some letters in it, well, that's because those are written in hexadecimal. So a hexadecimal A is 1010 in binary, and it's 10 in decimal. We're going to find out that 1011 in binary is 11 in decimal and B in hexadecimal, 1100 is 12 and C, 1101 is 13 in decimal, D in hexadecimal, 1110 is 14 in decimal, E in hexadecimal, and then 1111, all the bits are turned on, in decimal it's 15, in hexadecimal it's an F. That is the highest value we can have in hexadecimal. So when we get to a decimal 16, our binary is going to have to add a placeholder, so it's going to be 10000, and then hexadecimal is going to count up one value, it's going to add the 16s placeholder, and it's going to be 10. So this is not ten. This is 10 in hexadecimal, which is equivalent to a decimal 16. So 10000 in binary is 16 in decimal, which makes sense because we only have 1 bit in the 16s placeholder. In hexadecimal it's 10, and that's equivalent to 16 in decimal, and what that means in hexadecimal is we have the 16s placeholder and then the 1s placeholder. To wrap this up, what we did was we introduced the need for binary, learning that computers operate with these digital switches that can either be a 1 or a 0, so we need that binary, we reviewed some primary school math and just looked at how we count in decimal, adding those placeholders, and then we started a count in binary using the same method. Next, we converted some binary to decimal, then we did some decimal to binary, and then finally, we looked at hexadecimal and saw that each hexadecimal value is represented perfectly by four binary bits. I hope you found this very useful. Hopefully it wasn't too complicated of a math review. This is all the information we need to understand IP addresses, as well as MAC addresses later on when we talk about Ethernet.

## Chapter 11 IPv4 Addressing Fundamentals

Now that we know how to count in binary, translate binary to decimal, decimal to binary, and have a better understanding of hexadecimal, we can now move into IP addressing. So in the following chapters I introduce you to the IP address and we can see its components. First, we're going to answer the question what is an IP version 4 address? Next, we'll look at the difference between classful versus classless addressing. Next we'll look at different address types so that we can better understand how we use IP addresses. Then we're going to do a demonstration using IP version 4 addresses so we can see how they work and what rules we need to follow to make communication possible at the network layer. In the OSI model now, we are down at the network layer. We've covered application layer protocols like FTP and HTTP, we've talked about transport layer protocols like TCP and UDP, as well as how we address things at the transport layer, which was with port numbers. The port numbers at the transport layer were directly correlated with the application layer protocol. Now we're at the network layer, layer 3, and this is where we can talk about IP addressing. Internet Protocol operates at layer 3. So what is an IP address? The IP address is a mechanism for us to be able to communicate across long distances on the internet. The network layer address is much like your postal address, the address of your home or your business. It gives you a very unique, specific address on the face of the earth where anybody can send a message to you via that address. Same thing in Internet Protocol. The IP address is a unique identifier for your device on the public internet. There are routing tables on the public internet that allow anybody to communicate with your IP address, assuming they're able to find out what it is. Generally we find out the IP address of devices by using DNS. The network layer is where we use IP addressing to get messages from one device to another device on the internet. Here is an IP address, 203.0.113.10, and this address has two components to it. It has a network portion of the address, and it has a host portion of the address.

Network Portion    Host Portion

**203.0.113.10**

The network portion of this address is very similar to the ZIP Code of our street address. If we have the street, the ZIP Code represents an area of a city, and inside that area of the city we have specific street addresses. In this case the network portion of my IP address represents a group of network devices. The host portion of that address represents a specific device on that specific network. Just like a street address can identify a specific location in a specific area, 203.0.113 is our network, .10 is our host. It's a specific device on that network. So let's take a look at this a little bit deeper. Our IP address construction consists of four octets. An octet is just a set of 8 bits, and there are 4 sets of 8 bits in this address. We take each set of 8 bits, we convert it to decimal, and we separate them with periods, and this becomes our IP address.

# 203.0.113.10

11001011 00000000 01110001 00001010

This is not the best way to construct this. As a matter of fact, it makes for working with IP addresses a little bit messy, especially when we get into subnetting. But it's okay. As long as we understand that we can convert these 4 decimal values into 8 bits of binary, that's all we need to understand, because our IP address is really 32 bits long, and those 32 bits are one continuous string. The decimal points we only put there when we write it in decimal in order to make it easier to read and say. But how do we identify the network portion and host portion of that address? Remember we have that ZIP Code, the area of devices that are represented, the network portion, and then we have a specific host address? How do we identify where the network portion and host portion are? Well, we do that in one of two ways, and one of them is antiquated and we don't use anymore, and the other one is the only way we do it. So way one here is classful addressing, and we used that up until 1995 or thereabouts. The second method here is classless addressing, and that's what we use today, and we've been using that from 1995 until now. There was a transition period where it was a little messy, but now we exclusively use classless addressing. This can get messy, depending upon the network engineer you talk to because sometimes they talk about a classful subnet mask. Don't worry about that right now. What we're going to learn is how classless addressing works. We're going to do a review of what classful addressing is.

## Chapter 12 Classless & Classfull Addressing

This is what we use in modern networks. The way that we figure out which portion of the address is network and which portion is host is with something called the subnet mask. When we write our subnet mask, we're going to put a binary 1 in our subnet mask where we want the address to be network portion, and we're going to put a binary 0 in the part of the address where we want the address to be host portion.

**Network Portion**                    **Host Portion**

# 203.0.113.10

11001011 00000000 01110001 00001010

11111111 11111111 11111111 00000000

# 255.255.255.0

The subnet mask has to follow a set of rules that says the subnet mask is a series of 1s followed by a series of 0s. Wherever there's 1s, that's network portion; wherever there's 0s, that's host portion. Now we can identify which part of the address is network and which part is host. When I convert that to decimal, I get 255.255.255.0, and that becomes our subnet mask. 203.0.113.10 with a mask of 255.255.255.0. What that means is the first 24 bits are network portion; the last 8 bits are host portion. Understanding this division between the network and the host portion is really important, because it is literally how we identify where devices are, and there are rules about what devices can communicate with each other, depending upon the network portion of the address. Our subnet mask does not have to fall at 24 bits. Let's say we have this address of 10.0.0.10. If I convert that to binary, you can see my binary written out there, and let's say I want the first 8 bits to be in the network portion and the last 24 to be in the host portion. What I would do here is put eight 1s in my subnet mask, and then I'd follow it with 24 0s, and that would make a mask of 255.0.0.0.

**Network Portion**          **Host Portion**

# 10.0.0.10

00001010 00000000 00000000 00001010

11111111 00000000 00000000 00000000

# 255.0.0.0

You might be asking yourself, why am I making the first 8 bits network portion in the last 24 bits host? This at this point is purely arbitrary. I am making this up so you can see that our subnet mask can change, and when we change it, it changes which portion of the address is network and which portion is host. That's really all I want you to get out of this. Later on we're going to learn more about how to make subnets appropriately sized for the network we're working with. But more often than not, your job is not going to be to design the subnet mask. Rather, your job is going to be to use the subnet mask to figure out if an IP address is configured correctly and also better understand how the rules work. So let's look at another example here where the subnet mask is different. The subnet mask does not have to fall at an 8-bit boundary. There is no rule for that at all. Here we have an address, 10.0.0.10 again, but this time I have put the first 20 bits in the network portion and the last 12 bits in the host portion.

**Network Portion**        **Host Portion**

# 10.0.0.10

`00001010 00000000 00000000 00001010`

`11111111 11111111 11110000 00000000`

# 255.255.240.0

Now I have a subnet mask here of 255.255.240.0, and what this means is that the division between network portion and host portion falls right in the middle of an octet. This is 100% valid. There's nothing wrong with this. It makes figuring out what's happening with an IP address, especially when it's written in decimal, this makes it a little bit more complicated to deal with. The more you know about IP addressing, the better off you are in a career that involves data networking or network security because we can clearly understand when devices can and cannot communicate. We have an understanding now of how we divide our network portion and host portion using a subnet mask. Let's take a look at what we did initially. When IP addresses first came out in 1981, the design was that they would create 5 different classes of IP addresses, Class A, B, C, D, and E and they set up a rule to determine what defined Class A address, what defined a Class B, Class C, D, and E and here is the results.

| Class | IP Range | |
|:---:|:---:|:---:|
| A | 0.0.0.0 | 127.255.255.255 |
| B | 128.0.0.0 | 191.255.255.255 |
| C | 192.0.0.0 | 223.255.255.255 |
| D | 224.0.0.0 | 239.255.255.255 |
| E | 240.0.0.0 | 255.255.255.255 |

Class A goes from 0.0.0.0 through 127.255.255.255. B is 128.0.0.0 to 191.255.255.255. Class C is 192.0.0.0 through 223.255.255.255. E Is 224.0.0.0 through 239.255.255.255, and E is 240.0.0.0 through 255.255.255.255, which is the very last IP address we can have. These first three classes are called unicast addresses and these are the addresses we use on the internet and on our local networks in order to communicate. Class D addresses are for multicast. Multicast is when we have one server that sends out a stream of information and then there are lots of devices on the network listening to that. It's kind of like FM radio where you have one transmitter sending out a signal, and then you can have this little box, this radio, and you can tune in to that station and listen to it. There is no way to send a message back to that radio system back to the radio station, that's kind of what multicast does here. The last address range here, Class E, that is experimental and we don't use it. In classful addressing, the class of the address determines the division between the network and the host portion. So Class A addresses, the first 8 bits are network, the last 24 bits are host. Remember this is all historical. We don't use classful addressing anymore so this is purely historical and it's part of the Net+ exam.

**Class A:**    0.0.0.0 - 127.255.255.255

| 8 bits | 24 bits |
|---|---|
| **10.0** | **.10.10** |
| Network Portion | Host Portion |

00001010 00000000 00001010 00001010

You're also going to find some people talking about classful addressing and saying it's a Class A subnet mask. Well, okay, what that means is that there is 8 bits in the network portion, 24 bits in the host portion. Class B addresses are going to have the first 16 bits in the network portion, the last 16 bits in the host portion.

**Class B:**    128.0.0.0 - 191.255.255.255

| 16 bits | 16 bits |
|---|---|
| **172.16** | **.10.10** |
| Network Portion | Host Portion |

10101100 00010000 00001010 00001010

And then a class C address is going to have the first 24 bits in the network portion, the last 8 bits in the host portion.

Class C:    192.0.0.0 - 223.255.255.255

24 bits                          8 bits

# 192.168.0.10

**Network Portion**                    **Host Portion**

11000000 10101000 00000000 00001010

And then a class D address has all bits in the network portion effectively and this is our multicast addresses.

Class D:    224.0.0.0 - 239.255.255.255

# 224.0.0.6

**Network Portion**

11100000 00000000 00000000 00000110

Remember that classful addressing is useful to understand the history of this, but the reality is is we don't use that anymore. It was an antiquated way of handing out addresses and it forced the whole system to rethink how we hand out addresses in the late 80s and early 90's because no one really predicted the growth and the speed of growth of the internet, and had they not switched from classful to classless addressing, we definitely would have run out of IP addresses and the internet would not be what it is today.

## Chapter 13 IP Address Types

Let's talk about different IP address types here. There are a couple different types and a network address is an identifier for a group of devices - this is kind of like our zip code. This is also called our network prefix. So network address, network prefix, they're basically the same thing. The second IP address type here is a broadcast address and this is an identifier for all devices on a network. You might say, well if the network address identifies a group of devices and the broadcast address is an identifier for all devices on the network, what's the big difference here? The big difference is the network address is kind of like our zip code. The broadcast addresses is what a junk mail company might use to send you some advertisements to your home address. A lot of times it'll just say resident and it might just put a zip code on the address so that the postal carrier will put that same advertisement in every single mailbox in the entire neighborhood. The broadcast address is kind of like that junk mail you get, and it allows a sender to send a message to every single device in the neighborhood all at once. We don't use the broadcast address very often, however, we do need to understand that it is a type of IP address because we can't actually use the broadcast address to assign to a device. A host address is the third type of address here and it identifies a unique device on the network. This is most likely what you are currently familiar with because you may have had, at one point, to tell somebody, a technical support representative or a family member who is trying to help you, what your IP address of your device is so it identifies a unique device on the network and it's a combination of a network portion of the address and a host portion of the address where the host portion isn't identifying the network address nor the broadcast. Let's look at these three addresses in more detail. The network address follows a precise rule. It follows a precise rule and you kind of have to drill this into your head to make it work. Network addresses have all zeroes in the host portion.

## The Network Address

**Network Portion**                    **Host Portion**

# 203.0.113.0

11001011 00000000 01110001 00000000

11111111 11111111 11111111 00000000

# 255.255.255.0

So we look at the subnet mask, the subnet mask tells us the dividing line between host and network. We look at our IP address. If we have all zeroes in the host portion just like this address, that identifies a network address. The broadcast address is just the opposite, it is all binary ones in the host portion.

**Network Portion**                    **Host Portion**

# 203.0.113.255

11001011 00000000 01110001 11111111

11111111 11111111 11111111 00000000

# 255.255.255.0

Here we have our 203.0.113 address, our network portion of our address, and then if we put all ones in the host portion, then we get .255. This is our broadcast address, all binary ones in the host portion of the address. Remember, we identify the host portion of our address by looking at the subnet mask. Wherever there are zeros in the subnet mask, that is our host portion. If we put all ones in our IP address in the host portion, that becomes the broadcast address. The host address, which is the address that we can actually assign to a device that can't be the network address, it cannot be the broadcast address, but it can be anything in between.

## The Host Address

# 203.0.113.10

`11001011 00000000 01110001 00001010`

`11111111 11111111 11111111 00000000`

# 255.255.255.0

Here, if we look at the host portion of our address and we see that it is not all zeros and it is not all ones, that is a host address and we can assign that to a device on the network, it's anything, except all binary zeros or all binary ones in the host portion of an address. In this case, we have 00001010, that is not all zeros, that is not all ones. The secret here is making sure that we use our subnet mask simply to identify which portion of the IP addresses the host portion, and then when we are looking to see if it's network, broadcast, or host address, we are looking at the IP address and not the subnet mask. The subnet mask is just telling us where in the IP Address to look for all zeros, all ones, or anything, except all zeros and ones. The host address is what we assign to devices. Let's do some practice. 203.0.113.55 with a mask of 255.255.255.0. What kind of address is this?

# 203.0.113.55
# 255.255.255.0

```
11001011 00000000 01110001 00110111
11111111 11111111 11111111 00000000
```

If you convert this to binary, give that a shot. The answer here is if we convert that to binary, we look at the subnet mask to identify where the host portion is, we see that it is neither all zeros nor all ones in the host portion. This is a host address. Let's try another one. 192.168.10.25 with a mask of 255.255.255.0.

# 192.168.10.25
# 255.255.255.0

Write it out in binary. Here is the binary.

```
11000000 10101000 00001010 00011001
11111111 11111111 11111111 00000000
```

If we look in the host portion of the address, we can see that there are neither all zeros nor all ones. This is a host address. Let's try another one with 192.168.10.255 with a mask of 255.255.255.0. Is this is a broadcast address, network address, or a host address? In this case, we look at the host portion, we can see that 255 converts to 11111111, which is all ones in the host portion making this a broadcast address.

# 192.168.10.255
# 255.255.255.0

```
11000000 10101000 00001010 11111111
11111111 11111111 11111111 00000000
```

Let's try another one. What kind of address is this, 10.10.0.0, 255.255.0.0? In this case, we put it all in binary, we look at the host portion of the address.

# 10.10.0.0
# 255.255.0.0

```
00001010 00001010 00000000 00000000
11111111 11111111 00000000 00000000
```

You can see that it is all zeroes in the host portion making this a network address. You might be saying, these are super easy, why are we converting them to binary? And you may not need to convert them to binary to figure this out, but when we have a mask that doesn't fall on an 8-bit boundary, it makes it more complex. So how about this one, 10.128.224.64 with a 255.255.255.224 mask, convert that to binary and find out if it's a network address, host address, or broadcast address. When we convert that to binary, we see that the last 5 bits of the address are host portion, and if we look at the host portion of the IP address, we will see that it is all zeros making this a network address.

# 10.128.224.64
# 255.255.255.224

```
00001010 10000000 11100000 01000000
11111111 11111111 11111111 11100000
```

This is where things start to get a little bit messier if we look at them in decimal versus looking at them in binary. If we look at it in binary, the division line is pretty clear cut, you can see right where the ones end and the zeros begin in our subnet masks to find that dividing line. That's a little harder to do when we're looking at it in the decimal numbers. How about this one, 10.128.225.0 with a 255.255.254.0 mask. This is one that trips a lot of people up. Is this a network address, host address, or broadcast address? This also trips up a lot of people because the division between network and host portion is just one bit off of the 8-bit boundary for our decimal conversion.

# 10.128.225.0
# 255.255.254.0

```
00001010 10000000 11100001 00000000
11111111 11111111 11111110 00000000
```

When we're looking at this address, you can see that the host portion is the last 9 bits, and if we look at the host portion of our IP address, it's 100000000, that is not all zeros and that is not all ones making this a host address that looks a lot like a network address, but this is definitely a host address. So we have to be cautious when we're working with IP addresses to not jump to conclusions about what the IP address is. It's always important to convert this to binary, look at where the ones in our subnet mask tell us the network portion ends so that we can get a very clear understanding of what type of address this is. There's another way to notate the subnet mask and it's called CIDR notation. CIDR stands for Classless Inter-Domain Routing, CIDR, and we pronounce it like apple cider. CIDR notation here works like this. We have an IP address, 203.0.113.10 with a subnet mask of 255.255.255.0. If we convert that to binary, we see the first 24 bits of the address are network portion. What we can do is we can say, instead of saying 255.255.255.0, which is a mouthful, we can simplify this and say that any time we have 24 bits in the network portion, we can use Classless Inter-Domain Routing, or CIDR notation, and make this a /24. So a subnet mask of 255.255.255.0 is equivalent to /24, and this is just simply the length of the network prefix.

# CIDR Notation

Subnet Mask: **255.255.255.0**

11111111 11111111 11111111 00000000

**Classless Inter-Domain Routing Notation
or CIDR notation:**

Length of
Network Prefix ➡ **/24**

The first 24 bits of the address are network portion. The way we'd write that would be 203.0.113.10/24, and if we wrote it in binary, it would look just like with my IP address written out in binary and then the subnet mask having 24 1s with eight 0s at the end.

# 203.0.113.10/24

11001011 00000000 01110001 00001010

11111111 11111111 11111111 00000000

Next let's talk about private IP addresses versus public IP addresses.

| Private IP Address Range | |
|---|---|
| 10.0.0.0 | 10.255.255.255 |
| 172.16.0.0 | 172.31.255.255 |
| 192.168.0.0 | 192.168.255.255 |

Prior to 1994, there were no private IP addresses. We just had IP addresses. But because we were running out of IP addresses, we changed to classless addressing first, which gave us the subnet mask, and then we also introduced private IP address ranges. The idea was that any organization could use these private IP addresses. They would not be routed publicly on the internet, and it would allow organizations to set up very large IT infrastructures and very large networks using IP addresses without conflicting with other organizations. This is what saved the internet and allowed it to expand and grow as much as it did. We're later going to learn about a technology called network address translation, which allows us to take these private IP addresses, or large blocks of private IP addresses, and allows us to route out on the public internet by translating it into a public IP address for a moment while it routes across the public internet, and then it gets translated back into a private address when it reaches our internal network. The three ranges of address here, what they did was they picked ranges from each one of the classes. We have a class A here with a 10.0.0.0 through 10.255.255.255. We have a class B address, 172.16.0.0 through 172.31.255.255, and a class C at 192.168.0.0

through 192.168.255.255. This is all documented in something called a Request for Comments, or RFC. All of the protocols on the internet that we use, or nearly all of them, are written and publicly available via these RFCs. As a matter of fact, you can do a Google search for RFC 1918, you can click on the first one that's at tools.ietf.org. IETF is the Internet Engineering Task Force, and they are the maintainers and approvers of RFCs. Anybody can write an RFC and anybody can submit it. Whether it gets published or not is up to the IETF. Some of these RFCs have been out there for a long time and have never been approved. There are other protocols in RFCs, including IP. If we look for RFC for IP, we'll see that it is RFC 791, and that came out in September of 1981. If you look at that private IP address space with CIDR notation, we have 10.0.0.0/8, 172.16.0.0/2 and 192.168.0.0/16.

| Private IP Address Range |
|:---:|
| 10.0.0.0/8 |
| 172.16.0.0/12 |
| 192.168.0.0/16 |

There's also another network here called the APIPA network.

| APIPA |
|:---:|
| 169.254.0.0/16 |

APIPA stands for automatic private IP addressing. It's something that Microsoft and other organizations have

90

implemented. In my opinion, this should never be used. When you see a device with this address on it, it's an immediate red flag for me to know that somebody doesn't know what they're doing or something is broken. Boot up a computer and it gets this IP address, it means that something is wrong and it should be corrected. If you're using this address in your home network, you probably shouldn't do that. It's usually a good indicator to people trying to troubleshoot that something isn't configured quite correctly. We should definitely avoid using that space. There's another special IP address called the loopback address and it's 127.0.0.1, and we can send messages to this address. When we send messages to this address from our workstation, the messages never leave our computer, and it's generally a way to test to see if IP is working correctly on our workstation. In summary, we looked at what is an IP version 4 address, saw that it is a 32-bit number broken up into 4 octets written in decimal format. We looked at the difference between classful and classless addressing, noticing that we use classless addressing exclusively today, although sometimes you may hear people use the word classful subnet mask. We don't worry about that too much. All subnet masks are classless by definition. We looked at address types and saw the difference between a network address, host address, and broadcast address.

## Chapter 14 How to Subnet Networks

Now that we have a good understanding of binary, converting binary to decimal and decimal to binary, we've looked at IP addresses and understood how they're constructed, we looked at the subnet mask and learned how the subnet mask tells us which portion is network, which portion is host, now we can move on to this idea of subnetting networks. When we talk about subnetting networks, we're talking about subnetting IP networks from a large network into smaller components. Our goals will be first to review the address types. Next, we're going to break networks into smaller networks, which is the exercise of subnetting itself. We'll talk very briefly about Variable Length Subnet Masks, or VLSM. If you're working in IT, everybody should know this level of IP addressing. The math can get a little complicated, but with some practice, it ends up being not so hard. In order to have an IP network, we have three components to it. We have that network IP address, which is all binary 0s in the host portion. We have our broadcast IP address, which is all binary 1s in the host portion. These two addresses define the beginning and the end of a range of addresses in an IP network. Everything in between all 0s and all 1s is our host IP addresses, and these are the addresses we can actually assign to devices. If we take a look at our private IP space here, 10.0.0.0/8, we can rewrite this in the dotted decimal format of 10.0.0.0 with a 255.0.0.0 mask. Remember that /8 is just our

CIDR notation. This subnet is a very large subnet. There are 16,777,214 host addresses on this network. This, we could accommodate a very, very large network; however, we typically segment our network into smaller components, and I have never worked for an organization or saw an organization that had a /8 subnet that they were using for the devices on their network. They've always broken it up into smaller pieces. It makes it more manageable. Later on, we're going to learn more about Ethernet and how Ethernet works, and Ethernet really doesn't allow us to have 16 million devices on a single subnet unless we do some sophisticated things. So what we want to do is break this 10.0.0.0/8 subnet into smaller components. The range that we have to work with here is we can break this up in any way we want. We just have to stay within the constraints of 10.0.0.0, our network address, through 10.255.255.255, our broadcast address. Here that is converted to binary. And if I draw a line between our network and host portion, it'll be at the 8-bit boundary so that our first 8 bits are network, the last 24 bits are host portion.

`10.0.0.0/8`
`10.0.0.0 - 10.255.255.255`

```
N 00001010│00000000 00000000 00000000
B 00001010│11111111 11111111 11111111

  11111111│00000000 00000000 00000000
```

The best way I can describe how we're going to subnet this is let's find a host address on this network. I didn't pick this address arbitrarily. I picked it for a reason, and we'll see it in just a second. Here I have this host address of 10.0.10.0, and right now I have a /8 mask applied to it. So the first 8 bits are network, the last 24 are host still. We can tell that that is definitely a host address because if we just look at the host portion of the address, we can see it's not all 0s and not all 1s. Now what if I did this? What if I moved my subnet mask from /8? What if I moved it down over two /24 and I apply the /24 just to this single address of 10.0.10.0? Well, when I do that, now if I look at the host portion of my address, the last 8 bits, there's all 0s in there now.

```
    10.0.0.0 - 10.255.255.255
        10.0.10.0 /24
                 /24
                    |
N  00001010 00000000 00001010|00000000
```

Now suddenly if I apply a /24 mask, now 10.0.10.0 becomes a network address. Now you might be asking, where did I get /24 from? I literally just made it up. I pulled this mask out of a hat for this exercise to say, hey, we can take this /8 network and we can carve out multiple /24 networks. And all I have to do is pick an address here that has all 0s in the last 8 bits, like 10.0.10.0, apply my /24 mask, and now I end up with a much smaller network. As a matter of fact, this is a lot more manageable now because now I have from 10.0.10.0 through 10.0.10.255. This allows me for 254 different hosts. Zero to 255 is 256 unique addresses. If I remove two of them, one for the network address, which I can't apply to a device, one for the broadcast address, which I can't apply to the device, I end up with 254 addresses I can apply to host devices on my network. So now I have a carved out portion of 10.0.0.0/8. My 10.0.10.0/24 would be this small slice of it so here I have just a small piece of the 10.0.0.0/8 network. I don't have to use 10.0.10.0/24. I can actually use almost any combination I want as long as the last 8 bits of the address are 0 so that I can use that as the host portion of my addresses.

| 10.0.0.0/8 | | |
|---|---|---|
| 10.0.0.0/24 | 10.0.10.0/24 | 10.0.20.0/24 |
| 10.0.1.0/24 | 10.0.11.0/24 | 10.0.21.0/24 |
| 10.0.2.0/24 | 10.0.12.0/24 | 10.0.22.0/24 |
| 10.0.3.0/24 | 10.0.13.0/24 | 10.0.23.0/24 |
| 10.0.4.0/24 | 10.0.14.0/24 | 10.0.24.0/24 |
| 10.0.5.0/24 | 10.0.15.0/24 | 10.0.25.0/24 |
| 10.0.6.0/24 | 10.0.16.0/24 | 10.0.26.0/24 |
| 10.0.7.0/24 | 10.0.17.0/24 | 10.0.27.0/24 |
| 10.0.8.0/24 | 10.0.18.0/24 | 10.0.28.0/24 |
| 10.0.9.0/24 | 10.0.19.0/24 | 10.0.29.0/24 |

This is just a portion of what I can submit 10.0.0.0/8 into if I were to use a /24 mask. I can have 10.0.0.0/24, and that would be 10.0.0.0 as my network address through 10.0.0.255 as my broadcast address, and the next available network after that, or next available IP address, is 10.0.1.0 and then 10.0.2.0, 3.0, 4.0, and so on. We can continue to count these subnets up from 10.0.0.0/24 all the way through 10.255.255.0/24. All we're doing here with subnetting is we're breaking up this large network into a bunch of smaller ones and just counting them out. I do not have to always use a /24 mask. What I can do here is I can use different sized masks for different sized network applications.

**10.0.0.0/8**
10.0.10.0/24
10.0.16.0/22
10.1.0.0/16
10.2.0.0/30

Here with 10.0.0.0/8, I can have 10.0.10.0/24, 10.0.16.0/22, 10.1.0.0/16 or 10.2.0.0/30. These are all valid subnets of 10.0.0.0/8. There's some trickery to this though. We can't just randomly and arbitrarily pick IP addresses and masks and apply it to networks. We do have to make sure that there's no overlap between our subnets. This is called Variable Length Subnet Masking, and this is a more complicated way to do subnetting, but it is one that we see in the real world a lot. To wrap up what we've done here, we looked at the address type review and we reviewed that the network address has all 0s in the host portion, broadcast address has all 1s, and the host address is everything in the middle. I've repeated that a lot, so that must be important, right? Well, it is. Next, we looked at breaking networks into smaller networks, looking at that 10.0.0.0/8 network and breaking it into smaller ones. We looked very briefly at Variable Length Subnet Masks, or VLSM, to see that we do not have to apply the same mask to every single network.

## Chapter 15 IPv6 Address Fundamentals

So far, we've covered a lot about IP addressing, but that was all specific to IP version 4. Now we need to talk about IP version 6. This can be a little overwhelming at first, but we're going to find out that the rules between IP version 4 and IP version 6 are generally the same, we just have to deal with a new format of address that's much larger than our IP version 4 counterpart. Our goals will first be to review some terms to make IPv6 understanding a little easier, then we're going to talk about the difference between the size of the IP version 4 address versus the IP version 6 address. I'll then introduce IP version 6 addresses, we'll talk about how they're written and how we can simplify how they're written. We're going to look at how they operate and what rules they need to follow in order to communicate. We're going to look at different IP version 6 address types. There are more address types in version 6 than there are in version 4 and it has to do with some of the way IPv6 operates, which we're going to take a look at that, as well as how IPv6 gets addresses assigned to the interface. We actually have more options in IP version 6 than we did in IP version 4. Then we'll wrap this up by talking about IPv6 tunneling, which we can use when we have some IPv6 addresses on a network that we want to talk to another IPv6 network, but there is not an IPv6 connection between them. How about some terms here? Let's start with bit.

We've talked about a bit before. It is a single placeholder that can either be a 0 or a 1. A bit is a binary placeholder here. It can either be 0 or 1. If we have 4 bits, each 1 of those 4 bits can be 0 or 1. And when we have 4 bits, we have a term for that, and it's called a nibble. So, 4 bits is a nibble. A nibble can be written as a single hexadecimal value. Each hexadecimal value is written in binary with 4 bits. There are 16 different possibilities, and in hexadecimal, we count from 0 to 15 before we add another placeholder. Remember, we use letters for any number value above 9. A, B, C, D, E, and F are all hexadecimal values, and I've written it as 0xA. We can identify hexadecimal values often because there is a 0x in front of it that indicates that the number that follows that is hexadecimal. So if you encounter documentation and you see a bunch of letters and numbers written together, if there's a 0x in front of it, there may or may not be one, but if there is a 0x in front of it, that's definitely hexadecimal. Next, if we have 2 nibbles, that's 8 bits. Well, there are 8 bits in a byte. 2 nibbles is a byte, and a byte is 8 bits. So in our 8 bits here, we can assign that 8 bits any value we wish between all 0's and all 1's. If we were to write this in hexadecimal, hexadecimal now would be 2 hexadecimal values is equivalent to 1 byte of data. Here the number A8, the hexadecimal value A8, that is 1 byte worth of information, those are 2 hex values. Each hex value is 4 bits. You put them together, you have a byte. In IPv6, we typically work with values in 16 bit sections. So, this is 2 bytes, and we've coined the term hextet to represent 16 bits of data. So we're going to use our hextet here a lot in IP version 6. Hextet can be written as 4 hexadecimal values, which is equivalent to 16 bits. Each hexadecimal value, again, 4 bits, 4 times 4 is 16. Now that we have some terms out of the way, let's talk about the IPv4 and v6 address size. An IP version 6 address is 32 bits long. We write that as 4 octets, or 4 bytes worth of data. Each octet is 8 bits. We convert that to decimal to work with our IP addresses. This is unfortunate because IP addresses are much easier managed in hexadecimal, but we write them in decimal just out of tradition. If we convert that to binary, we can see that there are 4 sets of 8 bits.

## 32 bits long = 4 octets
## 192.168.10.10

## 11000000 1010100 00001010 00001010

That is 32 bits of address space. An IP version 6 address is 128 bits long. It has four times as many bits as an IP version 4 address. This is an enormous amount of bits for an address. We write that with 32 hexadecimal values, or 32 nibbles, and we separate it out into 8 hextets, and each hextet is separated with a colon.

# IPv6 Address Size

## 128 bits long = 32 nibbles = 8 hextets

2001:0DB8:0002:008D:0000:0000:00A5:52F5

```
0010 0000 0000 0001 0000 1101 1011 1000
0000 0000 0000 0010 0000 0000 1000 1101
0000 0000 0000 0000 0000 0000 0000 0000
0000 0000 1010 0101 0101 0010 1111 0101
```

So here, my IP version 6 address is 2001:0DB8:0002:008D:0000:0000:00A5:52F5. That is a mouthful. It is a lot to read off, and we're going to learn how to make this address simpler, actually. If we were to write out the binary for this, this number is quite large. If we had to convert these to binary all the time, this would get messy because it's 128 bits. It's a lot of binary values in order to write down to work with this address, which is why we work with it in hexadecimal. There's some other tricks here that are going to make it a lot easier to work with compared to our IP version 4 addresses with subnetting. In IP version 6, typically we use a /64 mask on everything. There are occasions when we don't, and sometimes when we look at routers and routing tables and things, we may see something different than a /64 mask. But when we're working with IPv6 addresses on our workstations, typically we're going to see a 64-bit network portion of the address, and then a 64-bit host portion, which we call the interface identifier portion in IP version 6.

| Network Portion 64 Bits | Interface Identifier 64 Bits |
|---|---|

```
2001:0DB8:0002:008D:0000:0000:00A5:52F5
```

So we have a network portion and an interface identifier portion. Our IPv6 address is messy to work with, to write down, to communicate to somebody, to enter into a device. There are actually some tricks we can use here to help make this address easier to read, write, configure, and work with. This looks a little daunting, and I realize that. Let's make it simpler. First thing we can do is we can eliminate leading 0's. So, when I say leading 0's, what do I mean by that? Well, in leading 0's, if I were to give you a dollar, or I were to give you $01 or $0001, all those are a dollar. It doesn't matter how many 0's I put before that 1, that does not change the value of the amount of money I'm giving you at all, versus if I were to give you a dollar and then add a 0 to the end of that, that will be $10, or add three 0's to the end of that, that's $1000, those are not all equivalent to a dollar. So if I put a 0 in front of a number, it doesn't change the value. If I put a 0 after a number, it does change the value. So, when we are working with our IPv6 addresses here, if I want to simplify this, I can take away any leading 0 in each hextet.

```
2001:0DB8:0002:008D:0000:0000:00A5:52F5
```

So here I have 2001, no leading 0's there, but 0 DB8, there's a 0 there that I can get rid of and just write as DB8; 0002, I can write that as 2; 008D, I can write that as 8D; 0000 I can write as a 0, and I can do that twice

101

here; 00A5, I can write that as simply A5; and then 52F5
are my last 4 hex values.

## Eliminate Leading O's

$$2001:DB8:2:8D:0:0:A5:52F5$$

So now I've simplified that address down. My 64-bit
boundary still exists here. I've taken some of the values
out, but each hextet here, every space between the
colons, is representative of 16 bits of information. So, I
can quickly and easily find the dividing line between my
network and interface identifier portions by just
counting the hextets. So I count 4 hextets, and that is 64
bits. Now, there's another way I can simplify this, and I
can eliminate series of 0's with a double colon, which is
just 2 colons side by side. So here what I can do is I can
take this series of 16 0's, and I can collapse that down
into a double colon. So here this long address that I had
in the beginning suddenly becomes
2001:DB8:2:8D::A5:52F5.

$$2001:DB8:2:8D::A5:52F5$$

And you may say, wow, that's still a mouthful and that's
still a lot. It is. However, what we're going to end up
finding out is that those first two hextets are typically
never going to change. So in our entire network
environment, all the networks are going to start with
2001:DB8, or whatever 2 hextets are assigned to your
organization for IPv6. When we're working with IPv6,
oftentimes the first 2 hextets are going to be identical

everywhere in your environment, so we're really just working with the last 2 hextets in the network portion, and then whatever interface identifier portion we have. The double colon typically is going to fall at 64 bits. It doesn't have to, but it typically does when we're working with IPv6 addresses. There's some potential errors here with the double colon. We can only use that double colon once in an IPv6 address, and the reason is that we have to know how many bits, exactly how many bits are being replaced with that double colon. We can only do that if we only have one of them, so we can know where it goes.

## 2001:DB8:2:8D::A5:52F5

Here, this is a valid IPv6 address, but if I do this one and I put 2 double colons in, I change the address a little bit here, so I have 2001:DB8:8D::A5::52F5, with double colons around the A5, I can't do this.

## 2001:DB8:8D::A5::52F5

My workstation and the network will have no idea what this means because I don't know if it means this, 2001:DB8:8D:0:A5:0:0:52F5, or if it means this, 2001:DB8:8D:0:0:A5:0. I don't know which one this this replaces. So we can't use an address with two double colons in it. Another one we have to watch out here for is if we forget to put the double colon in, in this case, we don't know where that double colon goes, so we have no idea where to divide the network and the host portion. We don't know what the host portion actually looks like. There's actually not enough bits here to make an IPv6 address. IPv6 is going to work very similarly to how we saw IP version 4 work. When the network portions of the address are the same, this means that these 2 devices can communicate with each other without any additional hardware. However, once I change one of the PC's to be on a different network, the devices are no longer on the same network, so now they can't communicate unless I add a router to the mix. When we are communicating between devices on the internet, the internet is full of routers that can route IP version 6. When we are communicating with devices on the internet, we are using something called IPv6 unicast addresses. IP version 4 has unicast addresses as well, and those were the addresses that fell in the old school class A, B, and C. Those are all unicast addresses. Class D addresses were multicast. So here in IPv6, most of our addresses that we're going to work with are going to be these IPv6 unicast addresses, and these addresses are used for global communication, and by global I mean communication on the internet with devices that are not local to your internal network. These addresses are for global communication. There are another type of address that we can have in IPv6. As a matter of fact, we must have this address to get IPv6 to work, meaning that every single device in our network is going to have 2 IP version 6 addresses. One of them is going to be the IPv6 link local address, and this address is used for local communication. It's always going to start with FE80, and it's going to have some identifier after that and this link local address allows IP version 6 to communicate with other devices on the local subnet. This address is used because IP version 6, unlike IP version 4, sends out periodic messages to find out who's on the network using IP version 6 to send out information about how to obtain addresses to send out information about what network, what unicast network they're on, among other things. It uses this link local network in order to communicate IPv6 information, and then we use our global unicast IP addresses to communicate with devices when we want to transfer data between our devices or out onto the IPv6 internet. In IP version 6, we have these unicast addresses, we have the global unicast address, and the link local address. These are both unicast addresses. The link local address, though, is going to have that FE80. It's going to have a mask of /10 by default, and that address is going to be automatically assigned to every single device that's using IP version 6. There's also a loopback address. there's an IP version 4 loopback address of 127.0.0.1. Here in IP version 6, it's ::1, which just means 127 binary 0's, followed by a single binary 1 with a /128 mask. So the loopback address is ::1. I don't expect you'll use that very often, but you may need to know what that is. The ones that we're going to be using most often when we're working with IP version 6, at least in modern current networks, is going to be these unicast addresses, both the global unicast address, which will let our device communicate with the IPv6 internet, and the link local address, which will allow our device to communicate IPv6 information within each subnet. There's a couple other address types that are important here. One is the multicast address. Multicast address is one to many communication. IP version 6 has capacity to open this up for multicast to be used on the public internet. In IPv4 we do not have a public way to use multicast addresses. All multicast is on a local network not connected to the internet. However, at some point in the future, we will have IPv6 multicast available to us. Another address that we have here is anycast addresses. Anycast is where we use 1 IPv6 address for many devices, and this allows for load balancing of devices on a network where we may have multiple servers serving up content to a user, maybe for a website, and we use anycast in order to route traffic to the lowest utilized server in our network. Likely, you will not encounter too many multicast or anycast addresses, at least not with the net plus certification. Once you get into more advanced engineering in IT, you will more likely see multicast and anycast being used. But, how many IPv6 addresses are there? The inventors of the internet had no idea that the internet was going to explode in the way it did. IP version 4 was written in 1981. In 1981, engineers then could conceive of the possibility that everybody, or nearly everybody on the planet would have a computer in their pocket that needed an address. So, how many IPv6 addresses are there? Well, engineers did not want to run out this time. So if we take a look just at the interface identifier portion of our address to tell us how many host addresses are available. Remember, there's still 64 bits in our network address; we're just looking at these 64 bits in our host portion or interface identifier portion. With 64 bits, there are 2 to the 64th possibilities. Two to the 64th is 18 quintillion 446 quadrillion 744 trillion 73 billion 709 million 600 thousand addresses.

Interface Identifier
64 Bits

:0000:0000:00A5:52F5

$2^{64}$

# 18,446,744,073,709,600,000

This is an obscene number of addresses. As a matter of fact, I can't wrap my head around that. I actually did some research to figure out what this means. What does this mean? What this means is that we could give to each star in the Milky Way galaxy 184 million IP addresses. If we did it for every insect on earth, we would get 2 IPv6 addresses for every bug. So, there's about 9 quintillion bugs on the earth, and we could give each of them 2 IPv6 addresses just for this 1 single network. Just for one single network, each bug could receive two. There's about as many grains of sand apparently as there are insects, so we could have each grain of sand could get two IPv6 addresses as well. This is just a really absurd way to think about it. To think that every single grain of sand could have 2 of these addresses, and we would only use up 1 single IPv6 network, it's really impressive how many addresses we have available. This is 18 quintillion host addresses for each IPv6 network. I don't expect that we'll ever use those up. However, it gives the engineer tremendous flexibility when designing networks.

## Chapter 16 IPv6 SLAAC & IPv6 DHCP

Now, let's talk about different mechanisms for IPv6 address acquisition. We've already looked at one of those, and that's to manually configure it. There's 2 other options we have here for IPv6. One of them is called SLAAC, which is actually stateless address auto-configuration. This is a feature that does not exist at all in IP version 4, but in IP version 6 it does, and the way it works is like this. Let's say I have a router, a default gateway in my network, and it has an IP address of 2001:DB8:4:A::1. What that router is going to do is periodically going to send out something called a router advertisement. In that router advertisement, it's going to advertise what network this particular segment of the network is. It's going to advertise the network address, so the IPv6 network address, as well as some other information that our endpoints or our workstations can use to automatically configure themselves without asking. What will happen here is we'll send this router advertisement, or RA, out into the network. That happens periodically, so we don't have to wait for a new device to come on. That router is just sending those messages out regularly. What will happen then is the workstation will then automatically configure its address. It now knows that it has network 2001:DB8:4:A with a 64-bit mask, and now the way that the interface identifier portion is configured depends upon the operating system we're using. If it's Windows, it's going to choose a random 64-bit interface identifier, so it's going to put our 2001:DB8:4:A, the first 64 bits, and then it's going to randomly assign the

108

next 64 bits of information to become the interface identifier. It's going to create two of these addresses to apply to our interface. There's always at least 2 addresses on our workstations in order for them to use IPv6. We can configure more than two addresses besides our link local address on those interfaces. When Windows chooses this random identifier, it chooses two of them and applies them to the interface. If we're on Linux or Unix or Mac systems, including a lot of smartphones, an Android, an iOS, it doesn't really matter, they're all one of these flavors of operating system typically, we're going to use something called a modified EUI-64 address. What we're going to do is we're going to take the MAC address of our network interface card. We talked about encapsulation, we talked about how at layer 2 we put all of our data in the payload and then we address it with a source and destination MAC address. MAC addresses are layer 2 addresses, and our hardware addresses for the specific network interface card that we're using, that could be wireless, it could be wired, and we're going to talk more about MAC addresses in the future, but for now, remember, that MAC addresses are layer 2. IPv4 and IPv6 addresses are layer 3, and then up at the transport layer, we address things with port numbers. Here with the MAC address, what we're going to do is we're going to grab that MAC address off of the network interface card, and we're going to split it into 2, and then add FF:FE in the middle. This will make the address 64 bits long. Traditionally, MAC addresses are 48 bits long, so by adding FF:FE in the middle, that adds 16 additional bits to our address, making it 64 bits.

### Unix/Linux/Mac
Modified EUI – 64
### MAC Address

### 000C:29 FF:FE FC:70A5

Now we have a 64-bit interface identifier portion, but with modified EUI-64, we do one more thing. We take the first 8 bits and we convert them to binary. Then, what we do is we take the 7th bit in that list and we flip it, so if it's a 0, we make it a 1, if it's a 1, we make it a 0, and then we convert it back to hexadecimal, and now this becomes the interface identifier portion for Unix/Linux/Mac workstations. We just add that into our network portion of 2001:DB8:4:A, and then the rest is basically our MAC address. The challenge with this is, is that if we're using the MAC address in our host portion of our address, or our interface identifier portion of our address, what this means is that anybody on the public internet that is receiving traffic from us will know what our MAC address is.

**2001:DB8:4:A:020C:29 FF:FE FC:70A5**

What we're going to find out is that that MAC address can identify the brand of the hardware we're using, as well as the device type if we have the right kind of table. We can figure out what computer somebody's using to connect to the IPv6 internet with this type of address. Although there is somewhat of a concern here from a security perspective, we don't worry too much about that in our day-to-day operations with IPv6. There are other ways to solve that problem, which we're going to look at next. Whenever we're using IPv6 SLAAC, once our router sends out that router advertisement, we then configure our address and then we send a message back out to the rest of the network saying, hey everybody, I am on the network now, this is my IPv6 address. Since some of those addresses are configured randomly, we're going to double check to make sure that no one else has that address. If somebody else has that address, there's mechanisms in IPv6 to sort out that duplicate address and have our workstation re-choose a new address. One of the ways we can solve the problem of using SLAAC and having it automatically configure an address using our MAC address is to use IPv6 DHCP. DHCP here is going to work very similarly to the way IP version 4 does. We're going to look more at DHCP services later on, but for now just know that, instead of the address automatically configuring itself, we add a DHCP Server into our network. When our device comes online, it's going to send out an advertisement saying, hey, I need an address and our DHCP Server will reply with one. In order to do that though, we do have to set our router up to turn off SLAAC, so that is a feature of IPv6 and we can actually turn it off in the router advertisement telling our client not to use SLAAC to configure itself and instead use the DHCP Server. This allows for a lot more control, it allows for shorter addresses, especially in our internal networks. There is a lot of value to using an IPv6 DHCP Server. Last thing we're going to look at is tunneling IPv6. One of the problems that we have with IPv6 is not everywhere supports it, not all ISPs have full support of it, it is not used globally in the same way that IPv4 is. Let's say that we have some IPv6 internet, locally and we want to connect to a device far away that has an IPv6 address. What would happen here is that in order to make this work, we're going to have to find a way to get our IPv6 internet traffic across the IPv4 internet and those 2 aren't backwards compatible with each other. What we do instead is we build something called a tunnel and a tunnel is nothing more than a mechanism where we can take an IPv6 message, an IPv6 packet, and we can put it inside of an IPv4 packet, move it across the IPv4 internet to another device where it will be pulled out of the IPv4 packet and then put back into an IPv6 message and it can be forwarded. This tunneling allows our IPv6 devices to traverse the IPv4 internet and access a device that has an IPv6 address. To wrap up what we've talked about with IPv6 as we looked at the terms for IPv6 talking about a bit, a nibble, a byte, and a hextet. We looked at the IPv4 address size, saw it was 32 bits and then compared it to an IPv6 address, which was 128 bits, 4 times as many bits in that address. We looked at IPv6 address operation and saw that it works very similarly to the way that IPv4 addresses work. We talked about IPv6 address types including the unicast addresses, both global and link-local. We also looked at multicast and anycast addresses. We talked about IPv6 address acquisition. Then we took a look at both SLAAC, the stateless address auto configuration, as well as IPv6 DHCP. We wrapped it up by looking at IPv6 tunneling. Let's move onto the next module where we start to get into some network services like DHCP, DNS, and NTP. We're going to look a little bit deeper at those protocols next.

## Chapter 17 Network Address Translation

Now we're going to discuss network services. Network services are functions on the network that end users typically don't know about. However, these services are critical to making networks operate correctly. So our goals will be first to talk about network address translation, or NAT. Then we're going to talk about dynamic host configuration protocol, or DHCP. We have talked about DHCP already; however, this time we're going to take a bit deeper dive into it. Next, we're going to talk about domain name system, or DNS. Again, we have discussed this briefly, but now we're going to take DNS to a deeper level and understand the terms involved in DNS and see how DNS actually works. Let's start with network address translation, or NAT. NAT is a network layer function, and we needed it in order to make the internet grow in the way that we use it today. Let's learn about how this actually works. At the same time that network address translation was written as a protocol, we also wrote the private IP address specifications where we set aside these three or four ranges of IP addresses to use on our internal networks, and these IP addresses cannot be routed on the public internet. As a matter of fact, if we send a message into the public internet with a destination address of any of these addresses that I've listed here, the internet will just throw it away.

```
10.0.0.0/8

172.16.0.0/12

192.168.0.0/16
```

All the routers on the internet are programmed to discard messages with a destination address of one of these ranges. But how does this work? Imagine that I have a small network in our internal devices. I've used the private IP range of 10.0.0.0 that I've subnetted into a /24. And then on the outside I have an address of 203.0.113.6. This is a public IP address. Let's imagine that we want to go on our workstation and browse to google.com. So if I were to generate a message, I would put a source IP address of 10.0.0.10 and a destination address of google.com at 8.8.8.8. I can then send that message out on the internet to Google's website, and it gets there just fine because my destination IP address is a public IP address, which is entirely routable on the public internet. However, when Google responds to my message, it's going to reverse the source and destination IP addresses, and this time the source IP address is going to be Google.com and the destination is going to be my workstation at 10.0.0.10. So when that message gets sent into the internet, the internet router is going to look at the destination and say, hey, 10.0.0.10, that's a private IP address, I can't route that. That can be literally anywhere on the internet, and it throws the message away now, and we can't get the message back to the destination. Instead what we do is we still create the same message where we have 10.0.0.10 as our source address, destination address is Google's website at 8.8.8.8. We send that message to the router, and when we get to the router, we have the router configured to do our network address translation. And what happens is the router will remove the source IP address from the packet of 10.0.0.10 and store it in a table. When we store it in the table, we put some other parameters in it to make sure we know exactly which packet this is for, and then we replace the source IP address with the IP address of the router at 203.0.113.6, which is a public routable IP address. We then forward that message on to the internet, Google's website receives it, gathers up the website, packages it up, and then it's going to send it back to us. Now it has a destination IP address of 203.0.113.6, we send that into the internet, the internet knows how to get to our router because it's in the routing tables of the internet. Once our router receives that message, it looks up in the little table that it's set up and says, this message, this is destined for 10.0.0.10. It then replaces the outside public IP address with our inside IP address of 10.0.0.10 and forwards the message on. This is how network address translation works. Network address translation is swapping out addresses in our packets in order to make those messages routable on the public internet. There's lots of uses for NAT beyond this, but this is the primary use of it. In our home networks, we're actually using something called port address translation. As we are in this setup here, I didn't get into all the details of that. If you want to see more of the details of network address translation, there's another course you can watch. Just know for this particular scope of content, network address translation is replacing IP addresses in our packets to make them routable on the public internet.

## Chapter 18 Dynamic Host Configuration Protocol

Now, let's talk about dynamic host configuration protocol, or DHCP. DHCP is an application layer protocol. The way DHCP works here is typically we need a DHCP server, a device on our network that can hand out addresses to the clients as they come online. There are lots of ways to do this. In large enterprise organizations, they will have a dedicated DHCP server that hands out the addresses for the entire organization, regardless if that organization has 100 devices or 50,000 devices. In your home network, typically that DHCP server is built right into the router. Let's talk about how this works. When we configure our device, we can configure our IP properties and say obtain an IP address automatically, and that's going to use DHCP to get that address. Our DHCP server then is set up with a scope. The scope is basically the parameters of DHCP. So here we're saying the scope is going to be for network 10.0.0.0/24, which is the subnet that I have connected to the router. We have a range of excluded addresses. This isn't mandatory, but oftentimes we put excluded addresses in our DHCP scope so that the server does not hand out these addresses, and we can use them either to statically assign to devices or to set up a reservation that's specific for a device. Usually these excluded addresses are reserved for static configuration, for things like servers or printers or other strange hardware that may not support DHCP very well. We need to include our gateway, or default gateway, or default router. All those are the same thing. We need to include that in our scope so that our devices know where the default gateway is so that when we're trying to send traffic off of our subnet, our workstations know how to route that traffic appropriately. We need to configure a DNS server like Google's at 8.8.8.8. Then we have a lease time, which is the amount of time that our workstations are going to hold on to that IP address before asking for a new one. If we want to get an address, our workstation's going to send out a message called a discover message, and that discover message is going to be received by the DHCP server. The DHCP server is going to make an offer to the workstation. So it's making an offer of 10.0.0.100/24. It's going to say what the default gateway is and what the DNS server is, as well as the lease time. That then becomes the IP address of the workstation. The workstation will then respond back to the server saying, hey, I request this address that you've offered me, and the server will send back a message that says I acknowledge that. We have a discover message, an offer, a request, and an acknowledgement. Now our workstation has this IP address, and inside our DHCP server, we're going to make something called a DHCP binding, and that binding is just going to be a table that lists out the address that we've handed out, along with the MAC address of the device that we are setting up. If we have a printer on our network, this is where the excluded addresses come in. We may need to have a static address assigned to that. We can do that in a couple of ways. We might pop that into our DHCP binding database, or we may just statically assign that address to that printer. The reason we need printers to have a static IP address is all the devices on our network always need to know how to reach that printer, so we typically statically assign that address to our device. In larger networks, we may have more than one subnet that we're working with, and in that case, our DHCP server can be someplace on the network and it doesn't have to be a local device anymore. What we would use here is something called an IP helper address. This IP helper address, what we're going to do is when we send out that DHCP discover message, when that message hits the router's interface, the router will say, oh, I know where to send this, the DHCP server is over here at 172.16.1.68, and it forwards the message across the network to a DHCP server that is someplace on the network that's not local to the subnet. This way we can have a single DHCP server for all of the subnets in our network.

## Chapter 19 Domain Name System

Next, let's talk about DNS, or Domain Name System, or Domain Name Service. This is another application layer protocol operating on transport layer 53, can use either UDP or TCP, depending upon what we are trying to accomplish. Typically, if we are just resolving a hostname into an IP address, we're using UDP. To start off with DNS, we first need to understand what a URL is, or Uniform Resource Locator. You may have heard of URL before, because this is what you would be given to visit a certain website. So if we wanted to go to Google.com, this is the URL, and it's broken into several components here, so let's take a look at what those are. First, we have the top-level domain, or TLD. The top-level domain is the last part of our URL, in this case, Google.com, the .com is the top-level domain. There are many top-level domains, including .com, .edu, .org, .net, .gov, .mil. There are country codes like .ca for Canada, .jp for Japan, .uk for the United Kingdom, .in for India, .au for Australia. And in the last 10 years or so, the governing body for these URLs introduced all kinds of new top-level domain names that you can purchase for your own organization. Just remember that that last part of our URL is the top-level domain. Each one of these top-level domains has a special service on the internet called a root DNS server that stores all the other URLs and tells them where the authority is for those particular domains. We're going to talk more about that in a little bit, but just know that each one of these has a special service running on a server on the internet that identifies where all the domains are and where we can find information about them for DNS. The second part is the second-level domain, and is our domain, or typically what we call our domain. So Google.com, that's our second-level domain and top-level domain. So then our second-level domain here is as much like google.com, cisco.com, wikipedia.org, he.net, facebook.com, and so on. That second-level domain is identifying the unique organization itself, or the unique URL for an organization's thing, whatever they're doing with this. Maybe they're setting up a special website, maybe it's for some services, like for an FTP service or whatnot. That second-level domain is typically identifying the organization itself, but it does not necessarily have to identify the organization, it's just a name that identifies a specific domain. Next, we have a third-level domain, and in the case of www.Google.com, the www is our third-level domain, and this is also the hostname of the server that we're trying to reach. So, www is a server at the domain Google at the top-level domain .com. So www is the third-level domain or the hostname, Google is our domain, and .com is our top level domain. That third-level domain doesn't always have to be a hostname. In this case, (www.engineering.univerisity.udu) we have a top-level domain of .edu, a domain of university, a third-level domain of engineering, which is a specific organization within the university. There might also be philosophy, and English, and literature, and physics, and chemistry, and what not. So every single department within a university may have its own third-level domain name where they can add then a fourth-level domain, which will be the hostname here, in this case, www is specific to a web server. When we are using DNS, the idea is that we need to have a DNS server configured on our workstation. Typically this is done through DHCP. If we take a look at our IPv4 properties, we can see that we can either manually configure a primary and secondary DNS server or we can ask our DHCP server for that information so that it's automatically configured.

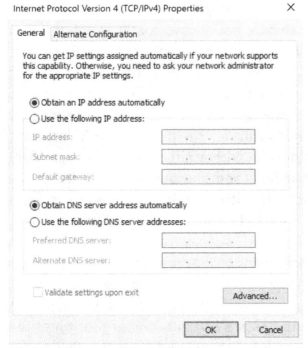

In this case, we have it automatically configure and our DHCP server is set to 8.8.8.8, which is Google's DNS server out on the public internet. So what I would do if I wanted to reach Google.com is I would type that into my web browser, but before my workstation could send a message to Google.com, it's going to have to do a DNS lookup, and what that means is that I need to send a message from my workstation to the DNS server that's configured on my workstation and say, hey, DNS server, what is the IP address of www.Google.com, and then the DNS server will reply and say, hey, Google.com is at 4.4.4.4. Then my workstation can create the packet and send the message to Google to get the website. We could also do a reverse DNS lookup. The reverse DNS lookup is going to say, hey, what is the domain at 4.4.4.4, and then the Google DNS server, if that record is configured, they're not always configured, but if that record is configured, we can reply back and say, hey, that's pluralsight.com. Our DNS can work in two directions. The primary direction, we're doing a forward lookup, we're saying, hey, what's the IP address of Google, that's what makes the internet work; however, if we want to do some other nifty utilities, we may want to take an IP address and find out what the URL or the domain associated with that is, the reverse lookups don't always work, because the record is not mandatory to have in DNS. First we have an A record. A DNS A record is an IPv4 record for a forward lookup. It maps a URL to an IP address. An AAAA record is an IPv6 record. If you remember right, IPv4 addresses were 32-bits long, IPv6 addresses are 128-bits long or four times the size of an IPv4 address, so, we just made the IPv6 record called an AAAA record, four As, four times as large. Next, we have a CNAME record, or a Canonical Name record, and this is a record where we can set it up in

DNS and there's no IP addresses associated with it, but what we can do is we can say if we go to this certain URL, redirect it to this other URL, and sometimes you see this happening, for example, with Google. If you accidentally mistype Google and don't put two Os in Google and instead type G-O-G-L-E and hit Enter, DNS will automatically redirect that to google.com with the correct spelling. Google purchased the gogle domain name and just put a Canonical Name record in DNS so that any time you try to go to gogle.com, it automatically redirects you to google.com with the correct spelling. That's a Canonical Name record. An MX record is a Mail Exchange record, this is what we're going to use when we're using email and our email client is going to do a DNS lookup for an MX record, so we know where to send our messages for certain domains. Next is an NS record, or a Name Server record, and this identifies an authoritative name server. On our root DNS servers, which are going to host our top-level domains, the .coms, the .edus, that service on those servers is going to host all these Name Server records, or NS records, and when we do a query, when we don't know what the IP address of a device is, we may have to go all the way up to the root DNS server, which we can say, hey, do you know how to get to Google.com? And that root DNS server will say, yes, I do, I don't have the address, but I can tell you where the authoritative DNS server is for Google, and it can redirect me to the right place so I can find out the records that I need. We have a PTR record, or a Pointer record. The Pointer record is for the reverse lookup. Earlier I said that we can do a reverse lookup where we put in an IP address and it tells us the domain associated with that. If we want that to work, we need to set up a PTR record or a Pointer record. There's also a Service record, the SRV or Service record, that is going to specify the IP address of that domain, as well as a specific port number to use if it requires it. The SRV record is specific for an IP address plus a port number. We also have a TXT record, and this is able to provide additional information about the IP address and URL association, if we need to send some specific information back to our clients about what this is, we can put this in human readable format. We can say, this is reserved for documentation, or this is reserved for this certain other thing. We can send information through DNS using this TXT record if we choose to. Let's take a look at how this works a little bit better by talking about internal versus external DNS, and we can talk about an example of what happens when we can't find a record in our local DNS server. In most organizations, we do not use this system where we're pointing to an external DNS server to resolve our hostnames or URLs into IP addresses. Instead what we have is an internal DNS server, and the internal DNS server serves many purposes, one, remember we're using private addresses in our internal network, and oftentimes we're going to have services and websites internally for our organization that require us to look up to an internal IP address or a private IP address, and in that case we are going to need to have an internal DNS server to do those lookups. What we would do here is we would configure our clients to look at the internal

DNS server to resolve internal hosts. Let's take an example, though, of if we're trying to reach Google.com. If I was trying to reach Google.com from my workstation, I would first send the request to my internal DNS server, because that's what would be configured on my workstation. If for some reason my internal DNS server does not know how to reach Google.com, what it will do then is it will be configured to search out to a public DNS server to get that information. It would then send that request up to an external DNS server, like Google. If for some reason Google does not know how to reach Google.com, what Google's DNS server would do is it's going to reach out to the root DNS server for the top-level domain of .com. The root server then would look up the authoritative name server and send the authoritative name server information to Google, so that Google's DNS server now knows where the authoritative name server for Google.com is. This authoritative name server is a service that will be run by Google, or more likely, contracted out to a third party to run the authoritative name server for Google, and that service then would have all of Google's domain name and all the hosts or third-level domain name information in it, so that any time somebody on the internet wants to reach one of those devices, it can go to the authoritative name server to look that up. Authoritative name servers never are alone or are almost never alone, there's almost always a secondary authoritative name server. The way that we get that to work is we'll configure the authoritative name server with all of our URLs and IP addresses, we'll do a zone transfer, and this is going to be using DNS port 53, but using TCP as our transport layer protocol as opposed to UDP, which we're using for all of our lookups. We do the zone transfer to our secondary server, that way if one of these servers goes down, we always have an authoritative name server to use. After the root DNS server tells Google DNS, the authoritative name server for Google is over here, now Google's DNS server can query the authoritative name server for Google, it can return the proper IP address to get to www.Google.com. Google's DNS can then report that back to our internal DNS server, and in that process, both the Google DNS server are going to cache that entry in a table and it's going to save that, so the next time somebody needs to look up Google.com, we can just look it up directly on our DNS server versus having to go to the root server, then the authoritative name server, and then back to the client that's asking for it. The Google DNS server is going to cache it, our internal DNS server is going to cache that entry for Google.com in its table, and it's going to then send that information all the way back to my workstation to tell me where Google.com is. It's only going to keep that entry in the table for as long as the TTL will allow it, and the TTL is the time-to-live. The TTL is configured by the authoritative name server in something called a Start of Authority record, or SOA. The Start of Authority record is something that the authoritative name server hosts, and it has configuration information including the TTL for that particular entry. The important part of using that TTL is that if we need to update the IP address of a server in our authoritative DNS server, we can force all of the other DNS servers to refresh their entries by setting that TTL to be very low, so that we automatically have to go all the way back up to the root server, then down to the authoritative name server in order to get the information. This wraps up us talking about some network services. We talked about network address translation and saw how it replaces IP addresses in our packet from private IP to public IP so that we can surf on the public internet. We talked about DHCP and saw how we can assign IP addresses to devices using that DHCP scope on a server. We also looked at domain name system and identified lots of terms in DNS in order to understand how that operates to allow us to have records that identify a host name, which is a readable name like www.Google.com in a URL and translate that into an IP address, which we can actually use in our packets to request information from those sites. The next place we're going to go to is talking about network topology, where I'm going to describe different types of network topologies, as well as introduce virtual networking and other terms.

# BOOK 2

# COMPUTER NETWORKING

### NETWORK+
### CERTIFICATION STUDY GUIDE FOR
### N10-008 EXAM

### BEGINNERS GUIDE TO ENTERPRISE
### NETWORK INFRASTRUCTURE FUNDAMENTALS

### RICHIE MILLER

# Introduction

The Network+ credential is the first certification that many IT professionals ever receive. It has been around for over 25 years at this point and has been awarded to over a million applicants during that time and this matter, because the certification has become well known by IT employers. When you're looking for a job and you have the Network+ after your name, most companies know that that's a real credential. It's also a vendor-neutral credential, in the sense that it doesn't promote any particular hardware or software vendor and although the exams do recognize and reflect the prominence of Microsoft Windows in the corporate world, they also include limited content on Apple operating systems, Linux, Android, and Chrome OS. Because Apple's operating systems only run on Apple hardware, the exams do cover Macs, iPhones, and iPads. It's fair to say that the CompTIA Network+ exams try to reflect the hardware and software that a technical support professional is likely to see in real life, and that's part of its relevance and appeal. In a nutshell, the Network+ certification is the preferred performance-based qualifying credential for technical support and IT operational roles, according to the organization that manages it, CompTIA. The Network+ certification focuses on the day-to-day work of an IT technician in a business environment. One reason the Network+ certification receives respect by IT employers is that it is accredited by international organizations. The ISO, or International Standards Organization, is a worldwide standard-setting group headquartered in Geneva, and ANSI, the American National Standards Institute, is the USA's representative to ISO. CompTIA has been accredited by ANSI for compliance with the ISO standard that applies to operating a certification body or organization, and CompTIA must maintain certain quality levels in order to maintain that accreditation. That's a bit of background on CompTIA and the Network+ certification. But who might benefit from this credential? Well, anyone wanting to be hired on by a company that requires it, certainly, but more broadly, anybody pursuing a career in tech support, for example, as a help desk analyst, service desk analyst or a desktop support technician. Field service techs will also find the credential helpful, as will those who aspire to being a network engineer or a documentation specialist in IT. This book will help you prepare for the latest CompTIA Network+ Certification, exam code: N10-008. First you will discover what are the most common Ethernet Cables, Coax Cables and Fiber Optic Cables that IT professionals use daily. Next you will learn about Multiplexing, Ethernet Fundamentals, CSMA/CD and Duplex and Speed settings. After that you will learn about Ethernet Frame Fundamentals, Ethernet Layer 2 Operations, Spanning Tree Protocol, VLANs and Port Aggregation. After that you will discover how to Route IP Traffic, how to use Address Resolution Protocol or ARP, how to Send Ping to a Default Gateway and how to build Routing Tables. Moving on, you will learn about Wireless Networking Fundamentals, specifically Wireless 802.11 Protocols, Wireless Ethernet Operations, Wireless Topologies and Management, Wireless Encryption and Cellular Wireless. Next you will discover what are the most common Layer 2 Devices and Services, what is Traffic Shaping and how you can discover Neighboring Devices. After that you will learn about Load Balancers, Firewalls, Voice over IP and SCADA Systems. Lastly, you will learn about Network Monitoring, Layer 2 Error monitoring, Facilities Monitoring and how to Baseline Network devices and services. As you can see, this book is a comprehensive guide on the CompTIA Network+ Certification and will reveal the must-have skills that every IT pro has. By finishing this book, you will become an IT professional, nevertheless, it is recommended to read the book or listen the audiobook several times to follow the provided guide. The audiobook listeners will receive a complementary PDF document, containing over 50 images; hence it's also advantageous to highlight critical subjects to review them later using a paperback or hardcover book, or the accompanied PDF once printed out for your reference. If you are a complete beginner, having limited knowledge or no experience and want to speed up your IT skills, this book will provide a tremendous amount of value to you! If you already working in IT but you want to learn the latest standards, this book will be extremely useful to you. If you want to pass the CompTIA Network+ Certification Exam fast, let's first cover what are the most common physical layer technologies!

## Chapter 1 Ethernet Cabling

First, we're going to talk about physical layer technologies. Our goals first to do a review of the OSI model so we understand where the physical layer is in relation to the other layers. Next, we're going to talk about physical layer medium options. The medium is going to be the stuff we use in order to send our signal. We're going to talk about two of the three options we have at the physical layer. We're going to talk about copper cabling and the specifications for it and then fiber optics and the specifications for that, including lasers. Then we're going to talk about Ethernet designations and how we call out the different types of layer 2 or data link layer Ethernet and how they need to use very specific types of cabling in order to achieve the speeds required. So let's get on with talking about the physical layer. Previously, we talked about the OSI model, and I gave you a general idea of what happens at each layer. As we progress, we're going to talk more about physical layer, data link layer, and network layer. We're going to focus mainly on the bottom three layers of the OSI model, and let's start with the physical layer here. The physical layer, we can have one of three different options in order to move data. One of those is copper cabling. It doesn't necessarily have to be made of copper. Really, the idea here is that it's going to be made of metal. But most of the cabling we use in most situations is going to be copper. Some friends have hacked around with using some technology to actually move Ethernet over train tracks, but that's a pretty unusual circumstance. So, we're going to stick with just copper cabling. The second option we have is fiber optics. Fiber optics is going to be a very thin strand of glass that we use a laser to shoot a type of light through. So it's actually photons that are carrying the messages that we're trying to send over our data network. The last option, which we're going to save for later on, is wireless. Wireless is also going to make use of photons in the electromagnetic spectrum. In this case, we're not going to have an actual physical thing that we use to send the signal. With wireless, we use an antenna, and we're going to use the electromagnetic fields to send a signal. We're still using stuff. It's just not stuff in the way that humans are used to seeing it, like we can recognize a copper cable or fiber optics. Copper cabling can be divided really into two different categories that we use in data networks. The most popular and most common that you will see, the one that you've likely seen in your home or in your office, is twisted pair cabling.

You can see the factory here where they're putting together some twisted pair cabling. You see all the spools of copper wire, and they're going to twist those all together and put insulation around it in order to make those cables. The second type of cable that we can use in networking is coaxial cabling. You may even have seen this too in your home if you have a cable modem, and there's actually some types of coax that we can use in data centers as well. Let's start by talking about twisted pair cabling. The reason that we use twisted pair cabling in data networks is to help increase the amount of data we can push through a wire. There's a physics phenomenon, that if you have a wire and you pass an electric current through it, that will create a moving magnetic field around the wire. Also, in the same way, if you pass a magnetic field over a wire, you will generate an electric current in the wire. That's how generators work. That's how we produce electricity. The problem in data networking is if you have two wires right next to each other and you put a current through one of them, the signal in the one wire will jump to the other wire very easily. We solve this problem in data networking by using twisted pair cables.

If you twist the wires together at very precise twisting rates, you can prevent that crosstalk, which is that signal jumping from one wire to another. If you look at this image, you can see that the pairs of wires that are twisted together in both the top and bottom images, you can see they're twisted together at different rates. You can see that the blue and white one is twisted together much more tightly than the brown and white one. Same thing with the green and the orange. They're all twisted together at different rates. By doing this, we create a cable that can pass lots of data at high rates of speed with minimal crosstalk and interference from other things. All these twisted pair cables are put into different categories. The categories have different specifications to allow for different types of Ethernet communication or different speeds of Ethernet communication. We start here with category 1 cable.

Category 1 cable is doorbell wire. It may not even be twisted. It's really not even networking cable. It's only worth talking about in the sense that it is category 1 cabling and is part of this system of cables for twisted pair. Second cable type we have is category 3.

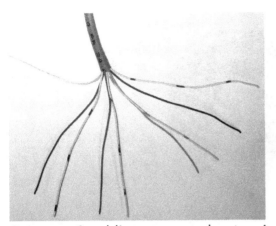

Category 3 cabling was used extensively for telephone systems, and these telephone systems eventually became repurposed for some use in Ethernet. We can run 10Mbps Ethernet over category 3 twisted pair cable. This was real convenient back in the late '90s when data networks were just becoming popular. Most office workers did not have a computer at their desk in the mid to late '90s. As a matter of fact, you have to be in a very special office setting, oftentimes, in order to have a computer at your desk. When you did, it was usually using 10Mbps Ethernet. Usually, in fact quite likely, you didn't even have internet at your desk in the late '90s. At the time, 10MBPS Ethernet was just fine in order to achieve what was necessary for file sharing or maybe email in those days. But as time evolved, we needed faster data networks to move bigger files. In that case, we came up with category 5 cabling, which just had tighter specifications on the wire itself, and it allowed to pass traffic at 100 Mpbs using Ethernet.

Shortly after that, we came out with category 5E. Category 5E is difficult to distinguish from category 5, but the idea here is that we increased the specifications in the manufacturing process to make sure those twists were twisted together at very precise rates.

Everything about the cable was made in a more precise way in order to get those higher speeds. The same thing happened with category 6.

We increased the specifications and also added this little plastic spacer in the middle of the wire. That plastic spacer keeps those four pairs of wires very well separated in the exact way that's necessary in order to pass traffic at a faster rate. This eventually led us then to category 6A and category 7cabling, which allows us to pass 10GB Ethernet over it, so 10 times as fast as we can get with category 6.

The idea here again is that we're just using more precise specifications when we're making the cable in order to achieve those higher data rates. There's another thing we can add to each of these categories of cables, and that is shielding.

We see unshielded twisted pair, or UTP. This is likely what you're going to see most often in the real world. We're going to just have a cable, and you're going to cut it open in order to put an end on it or attach it to a patch panel, and there's going to be no metal shielding around it. However, if we're in an environment with lots of electromagnetic interference or radio frequency interference, meaning we run these cables past fluorescent lights or they might run past a very strong radio transmitter, we don't want those signals from the lights or the radio transmitter to accidentally corrupt the signal that's traveling through the wire, which can easily happen. What we can do in the cases where we need it is we can use shielded twisted pair, or STP. The shielded twisted pair here helps prevent a lot of interference from external sources of electromagnetic interference, which brings me to category 8 cabling, which is special.

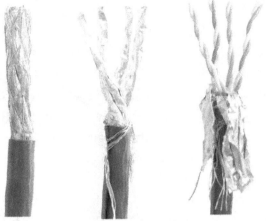

It has other restrictions on it that the other cables don't have. It can't necessarily go the same distance, and it has a different connector type that it uses. We're going to talk about connector types in just a bit. But with category 8 cabling, you can see that it's shielded. There's a wire mesh around all the cables. Then around that wire mesh is some more shielding around each individual pair of wires. Category 8, we're likely not going to see that used going to your desktop. However, you will likely see that used in data centers for special applications requiring 40GB Ethernet, which is just blazing fast. When we talk about categories of cabling and what type of Ethernet can run on it, this is how we label this. We have 10BaseT and then CAT3 cabling. Remember in CAT3 cabling, I said the maximum speed of Ethernet is 10 Mpbs. Ethernet designation, 10BaseT, that means 10 Mpbs using base band, which we're not going to worry about right now, and the T stands for twisted pair. So we're doing 10Mbps Ethernet over twisted pair, and that's using CAT3 cabling. If we look at the next one, 100BaseT. That is 100Mpbs Ethernet using twisted pair cabling. It's going to be category 5 cabling there. 1000BaseT, that's a gigabit per second. Twisted pair cabling. That's CAT5E or CAT6. 10GBaseT or 10GB Ethernet on twisted pair can use CAT6A or CAT7. 40GB Ethernet on twisted pair is what we need CAT8 for. When we look at these twisted pair cables, if we're using a telephone system, we're going to use something called an RJ-11 connector. That's just a little four-wire connector, which looks very similar to this RJ-45 connector, which we see on Ethernet cables or twisted pair cables. One of your jobs might be, as a network technician to replace these cable ends.

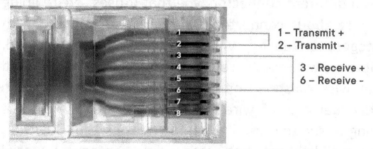

1 – Transmit +
2 – Transmit -

3 – Receive +
6 – Receive -

When we're looking at how these cable ends are specked out, the pins are numbered. If the clip is behind you and you have it positioned exactly as I have it shown in this picture, pin 1 is at the top, pin 8 is at the bottom. We typically only use four of the wires to actually transmit data. The other four wires are still needed, but they actually don't pass data networking traffic typically. We just need them connected to make the cable work correctly. Pins 1 and 2 are they transmit wires. Pins 3 and 6 are the receive wires. The other pins, 4 and 5 and 7 and 8, those are not used, but they do need to be connected. You can kind of see through the connector. You'll notice that the pair of wires that's white-orange and orange are connected to pins 1 and 2. And you can't really make out the color of pin 3's wire. But if you look down at pin 6, you can see that it's green, and that means that pin 3 is going to be white/green. So it's very important that we get the pairs of the wires correctly in order to make this cable work as efficiently as possible. If you don't get this right and you don't get the order of these wires correctly connected to the right pins, you can reduce the capacity of the cable by 70, 80% or more even. We really want to make sure that these pins are configured correctly in order to get our cables to work right. The specification we use in order to do that is one from EIA/TIA, and it's 568-B. We're going to look at 568-A as well in just a moment here, but the ones that we use for most cables when we're putting the ends on a cable is 568-B. And what that means is pin 1 is white/orange, pin 2 is orange, pin 3 is white/green, pin 4 is blue, pin 5 is white/blue, pin 6 is green, 7 is white/brown, and 8 is brown. We want to make sure we get these pairs of wires, and the exact right pin number in our jack to meet our specification. The category 5/6/7 cabling color, we have the four different colors with its white paired colors, so orange/white/orange and so on. When we hook them up to our straight through cable using 568-B, we can see that we have white/orange/orange. And then pin 3 is white/green, and pin 6 is green.

This is a straight through cable. This is used for most applications. We can also make something called a crossover cable. The crossover cable here, what it will do is it will take the transmit wire of one end of the cable, and it will connect it to the receive end of the other end of the cable.

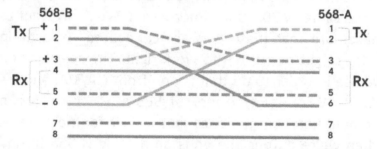

When we do this, we put 568-B specification on one side and 568-A specification on the other side. You might be saying, you just told us a messy story here about a straight through and a crossover cable and how they're built, but we don't know how they're used. I understand that. These cable types, straight through and crossover cables, you need to know the difference between these two and where they're used and which specification goes at each end of the cable for each one. So a straight through cable is going to be 568-B on both sides. A crossover cable will have 568-A at one side and 568-B on the other side.

**Straight Through Cable**　　**Crossover Cable**

We can tell the difference between a crossover cable and a straight through cable by comparing the RJ-45's end side by side. In our straight through cable, it should be white/orange and orange on pins 1 and 2, which are the leftmost pins in this picture. In our crossover cable, we should have white/green and green on one side and white/orange and orange on the other side. When we use these cables, we want to use a crossover cable when we're going from like device to like device, so router to router. In a router to router or a switch to switch scenario we use a straight through cable and if we have PC to PC, we're going to use a crossover cable. Let's mix this up and do a couple other examples here. When we're going from a PC to a router, this is one weird case where we use a crossover cable. Routers are kind of like a PC. It's kind of like a server that does routing of data network traffic. So it's kind of like a like device to a PC. But when we go from a PC to a switch, that is a straight through cable. When we go from a switch to a router, that's a straight through cable, and the real truth of the matter here is is that almost all modern devices, almost all modern devices, use a technology called Auto-MDI-X, which is auto-medium-dependent-interface crossover. I don't expect anybody to remember all what that word means. But if you hear somebody say, oh, Auto-MDI-X is on there. You don't need to worry about the cable. What that means is that you can use any cable, a crossover or a straight through cable, to connect two devices together, and the network interface cards, or NICs, on those devices will automatically figure out if it needs to be a crossover or a straight through, and it'll electronically reassign the pins for us.

## Chapter 2 Coax Cabling and Cable Termination

Another one that we need to talk about here now is coax cabling. The coax cabling that you're likely most familiar with is the one that comes into your house that either provides you cable TV if you still have that or cable internet.

This is going to use an RG-6 cable and that RG-6 cable is going to use an F-type connector. So that F-type connector is the screw-on connector with the wire sticking out the middle. That wire sticking out the middle is what we use for carrying the signal. There's some shielding on that cable as well. And we can use that to provide cable internet and cable tv. Another type of coax cabling that you'll likely see in a data center that can transmit data at 10 GB or 40 GB even is something called a twinaxial cable or twinax.

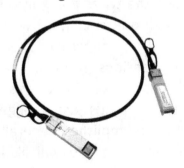

Twinax, you'll often see, it'll come with the network interface cards built right into the cable. That's what we're looking at there. Those are called SFPs. We'll learn a little bit more about SFPs when we talk about fiber optics. But here with the twinax cable, we might use this in a data center to connect switches or routers or servers or storage area networks together. These can be a little bit less expensive than using a fiber optic system. If you're working with very old school technology, especially old school telephone systems, you may never encounter this at all. But if you do work in an environment where they're using very old school telephone systems yet and they're not on Voice over IP, you might encounter something called a 66 block.

A 66 block is a bunch of connectors here where we can push one of our twisted pair wires into it, and it connects them together. In this block here, each row of pins or jacks there that you see the wires going into is all connected together, so it's all one circuit. So when we do this, we can actually hook together phone systems doing this and create extensions. You won't see this in data networking at all. Another version of this is something called a 110 block, and that's just a bigger version of the 66 block, and it accomplishes generally the same exact thing. Something that you will likely encounter in the field if you are working on cabling is something called a punchdown tool, and this is a punchdown tool.

The end on the punchdown tool is the important part. The punchdown tool is a little bit spring-loaded. So as you push it, when you get to the end and you're pushing the wire into one of those blocks or some type of patch panel, the spring will pop, and it's going to actually cut off the wire. You should notice on the image that there is a little wedge at the end of that punchdown tool. This tool is going to allow you to push a wire into one of those punchdown blocks, and then it'll cut off the excess wire as you do it to make a nice clean install. Those ends on this punchdown tool can come in one of several different types. One is called Krone, one is called 110, and another one is called Bix. Those are for just different systems of pushing wires into some type of patch panel. Here is a patch panel that is not connected to a rack at this point.

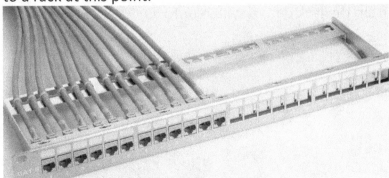

But the patch panel is a place where you would run the cables from some central location where like a switch is to each individual desktop or each individual server in an office building or in a data center.

If you look at the backside of that patch panel, what you'll see is a bunch of punchdown locations. Here, you can see there's like some white strips with colors coded on them, and those colors represent each of the pairs of the twisted pair cabling. What you'd do is you'd cut open the cable, cut open that twisted pair cable, and then run each wire to the correct spot in that punchdown panel or in that patch panel. Then you'd use your punchdown tool to push that wire in there securely and cut off the excess. That's how we use the punchdown tool to push these wires into those jacks, and then we can connect a patch cable at the other end from the jack onto a switch or to a PC.

## Chapter 3 Fiber Optics

Fiber optics are really nifty stuff. They're really, really cool. What we do is we take a very thin piece of glass. It can be as thin as your hair or thinner, and we wrap it in lots of insulation and armor to protect it. The fiber optic cabling itself can be relatively thick compared to the actual fiber that's going through it. The whole reason we make it thick is to prevent that cable from getting damaged. There's two types of fiber optic cabling that we can use, and the different types have to do with the thickness and quality of the glass used in the fiber.

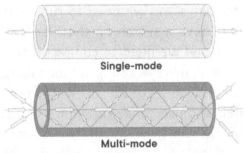

Single-mode

Multi-mode

The top one - the single-mode fiber, that fiber optic is very, very, very thin, has very, very tight specifications for the quality of glass used, and when we send laser light through it, it takes a very straight path through the glass, there's very little attenuation, or loss of signal, as the laser passes through the fiber optic, which means that single-mode fiber can go very long distances. Multi-mode fiber is a slightly lower quality glass, and is a slightly thicker fiber optic, which makes it cheaper to make, which means that we can use it in applications where we don't need to go 10 km, maybe we only need to go 1 km, and we can use multi-mode fiber then, which is a more economical way to do this. When we pass laser light into the multi-mode fiber, it has a tendency to bounce around the sides of the fiber optic a lot more, which can attenuate the signal, or reduce the strength of the signal, as it moves farther and farther down the cable. Single-mode fiber we use for long distances, multi-mode fiber we use for shorter distances when we can because it's less expensive. Single-mode fiber characteristically has a yellow jacket around it. Multi-mode characteristically has an orange jacket around it. Sometimes multi-mode fiber, as we'll see later on, will have an aqua jacket around it as well, depends upon the speed of Ethernet we're using with it. Where do we use single mode versus multi-mode? If we have two office buildings and we need to run some data networking, we may have a switch on the first floor of each of these buildings and we need to connect it to a switch on the top floor. Well, if we're using copper cables, there's a limitation. We can only go 100 m. If it's more than 100 m, we are unable to use copper anymore unless we put in a repeater, which is messy, or otherwise, we're going to have to use fiber optics. Typically, we would use multi-mode as our next option. With multi-mode fiber, what we could do is we could connect the switch on the bottom of the office building to the switch on the top of the office building using multi-mode fiber. If we want to connect these two buildings together, we can use single-mode fiber, assuming these buildings are a couple miles apart or 10 kilometers apart, we can use single-mode fiber to connect these two buildings together. Oftentimes, we're using multi-mode fiber within a building, or maybe on a campus where buildings are very near each other, and then we'll use single-mode fiber when the buildings are far apart and we need to transfer the signal for long distances. Some specifications on single mode versus multi-mode fiber optics, the laser type that we typically talk about when we're using single mode is LX or LR. When we're talking about multi-mode, it's SX or SR. The way I remember those in my mind is the L stands for long haul, the S stands for short haul. So if we need a long distance, we're going to use single-mode fiber, that's LX. If we needed shorter distances, that single-mode fiber, that's SX. The wavelengths of light here involved with the lasers, the most important part here is that, knowing just that there's different wavelengths of lasers that we're going to use here. These wavelengths of lasers we use are not actually visible to the human eye, however, they can damage the human eye. We're going to take a little bit deeper look at that in just a second here. Some of the optical network interface cards that we use, these optical network interface cards, sometimes they're called optics, sometimes they're called lasers, sometimes they're called a NIC. Just know that when we're talking about fiber optics, we're going to use lasers to light up the fiber and transfer the data. Here are two different types of laser modules we can use.

One is super old school, it's a GBIC, you can even see on that GBIC it says MULTI-MODE 850 nm November 2003.

It's a pretty old device there. You're not going to see many of those GBICs used anymore. You're much more likely going to see a small form pluggable, or SFP. The next generation of those are called SFP+, with a little plus sign next to them. They look exactly the same as what you see here in this picture, and they plug in to a special interface on a switch, or server, or other network device. As technology moves forward, we're going to see faster, and faster, and faster communications. Here is some for QSFP and QSFP+.

You should be able to recognize the SFP, the small form pluggable there, but the difference here is these are quad, so Q is for quad, or four, so these actually are four times the speed of a regular small form pluggable. Those all come in different speeds and have different characteristics. This is likely a 40 GB connection here and it's using multi-mode fiber. If you remember earlier, I said sometimes the multi-mode fiber has an aqua colored jacket, or this blue/green colored jacket, and that indicates that it's using a high-speed network interface card or high-speed lasers. In this case, the QSFP or QSFP+s. Here's an image of a GBIC in a very old device.

This is a Catalyst 3500 switch. These are not made anymore. So you may see some legacy gear in your network. Maybe there's a system that just can't be touched and it's been running for decades, and you might see something like this where there might be a multi-mode laser or a single-mode laser in there in the form of a GBIC, but it's likely going to be uncommon in modern networks. The connectors we have here, we have the ST connector, that's going to be a round-type bayonet connector.

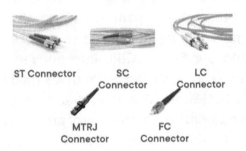

ST Connector     SC Connector     LC Connector

MTRJ Connector     FC Connector

We have an SC connector, and that is going to be a square-type connector where each fiber in the pair gets its own large connector that we plug into. We have LC connectors. These are very common in modern networks. It's a small connector that plugs into an SFP. And then the bottom two, the MTRJ and the FC connectors, you're likely not going to see those in the real world unless you're looking at a very old or very specialized application. These connectors plug into patch panels. So here's a patch panel.

Our patch panel is likely going to be in our data centers or in some central location. If it's a large office building, maybe all of the fiber optics are going to come into one central room, and then we can connect all those to switches. The reason we do this is we don't want to plug the fiber optic that's running through the walls right into our switch. We tend to plug and unplug at the switch more often than anywhere else. So what we do is we terminate the fiber on these patch panels, and then we use a shorter piece of fiber to plug into the patch panel so that we can plug it into our SFP or GBIC into our gear. When we're plugging these in, the connection that's made is they have to actually butt those little individual hairs of fiber optic glass right up against each other very precisely. These connectors, its intention is to align that very, very precisely, and then we use a special type of contact there. The ends of the fiber optics are polished, sometimes at this angle, it's called an angled physical contact, so that when the connector pushes together, it pushes that fiber optic together so that it has that angle that connects it together, and this makes it very easy for the light to flow through that without losing much light. Any time we have a connection or a break in the glass and we have to fix it, or patch it, or make some type of joint on it, we're going to lose some of the power of the signal through that joint. When we have something like angled physical contact, that helps improve that connection to make that low loss. Another type we have here is ultra physical contact. The way we do this is we put a chamfer on the ends of the fiber. This is really minuscule sized. This is very specialized equipment that's making these connections. Then when we butt the fiber together and we pass a light through it, we have a nice, clean connection where we have very low loss of light with this ultra physical contact connection. Whenever we're looking at fiber optic operation, were almost always using two fibers to achieve the connection; one is for transmitting information from one device to the other and the other is for the other direction. In this type of communication, this is called simplex or simplex pair. Like one end of the connection on that top fiber, the laser, is on the switch on the left, and then there's an eye for receiving that laser on the switch on the right, on the top fiber. Then on the bottom fiber, it's flip-flopped, where the switch on the right has the laser and the switch on the left has the eye for watching that signal come in. In specialized applications, especially in internet service providers that are providing fiber optic to the house, we would use bidirectional communication here, which means that the lasers, the optics that we put at each end of this, are going to be able to send light into the fiber, as well as watch light that's coming through the fiber. Because we're using one fiber, what needs to happen is we need two different wavelengths of light in order to accomplish that. In order to do that, we use something called WDM, or wave division multiplexing. We can actually use this wave division multiplexing in multiple operations. A single piece of fiber like this, I actually looked at the fiber into my own home for my fiber optic internet connection, and there's only one fiber coming into my house. It's just a single fiber optic strand that's connected to a laser that can both send and receive data. They do this because it's a lot more cost saving for an organization, like an internet service provider, where they have fewer network interface cards to buy and they can have less equipment in order to support this, especially when there's lots of customers on a single area. Just like designations for Ethernet, when we talked about using twisted pair, we have the same thing happening in fiber optics. We're using either multi-mode or single-mode fiber. The top one, 100BaseFX, you're probably not going to see that much anymore, but that's going to use multi-mode fiber. That's 100 mbps using multi-mode fiber. 100BaseSX, that's using multi-mode fiber. You may not see that either, but you will likely see somewhere in your career, 1000BaseSX, that's going to be a gigabit Ethernet connection using multi-mode fiber. Then we have gigabit LX, using single-mode fiber, long haul. We also have 10GBaseSR. The SR here is going to be 10 Gb. It's going to be multi-mode fiber and it's likely going to be the aqua-colored fiber versus the orange-colored fiber that we would use in the other types here. Then 10GBaseLR. LR here again, long haul, that's going to be using single-mode fiber in the yellow jacket. This is going to be all 10 Gb.

## Chapter 4 Multiplexing Fiber Optics

Multiplexing is a way where we can take multiple wavelengths of light and put them on the same fiber optic cable. The way this works is here's the electromagnetic spectrum.

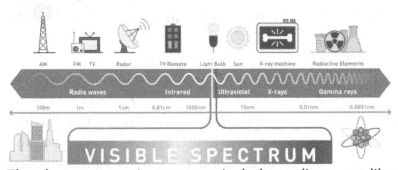

The electromagnetic spectrum includes radio waves like AM/FM radio and TV, radar, the infrared from your TV remote control or heat lamps when you go to a restaurant and they have food sitting under heat lamps. It includes the visible light spectrum which is the ROYGBIV rainbow. We have ultraviolet light that gives us a suntan. We have x-rays that we use to appear into our bodies. And then as we go on from there, we have gamma rays and other types of rays. These types of waves in the electromagnetic spectrum are actually dangerous to humans because the wavelength on there is very tiny, smaller than the size of an atom, and it can actually knock parts of the atom off and cause severe issues, especially for living creatures. The idea here is that the electromagnetic spectrum is a bunch of waves, electromagnetic waves, that have different wavelengths. On the left-hand side, those are very large wavelengths, 100 m or more. At the visible light spectrum, we're in the nanometer area. Then over towards gamma rays, they're very, very, very tiny, the tiniest size being smaller than an atom. When we look at what we're using for fiber optics, we're using a part of the spectrum that's right here on this orange line, and that's part of the infrared spectrum. We can't see it with our human eyes, but it will burn our retinas if we shine it into our eyes. The idea here is that we're going to use multiple wavelengths and combine them together on a single fiber optic cable. Well, to do that, we're going to use prisms. You may have seen a prism used to create some rainbows. You just shine a white light through the prism, and it creates a rainbow, and that rainbow is nothing more than the light separated out into its individual wavelengths. What we can do is if we shine a light into the prism, it's going to create a rainbow for us. It's going to separate those colors out, even the stuff that we can't see with our own human eyes. If we shine some rainbow light into a prism, we can have it output a single stream of white light. The idea here now is that if we have three different lasers and we shine them into a prism, that prism can combine all three wavelengths into one single light that we can send through our fiber optic cable. Then at the other end of the cable, we can send that through a prism again, and it'll separate out that light into its individual colors again. This is really, really nifty technology, and it allows for us to have very high-speed fiber optic connections of 100 GB or more. These are extremely fast connections that can go very long distances. Those can go from 1 km up to 70 km and even more if we have the right kind of gear. There's two different types of multiplexing we can use. One is called course wave division multiplexing or CWDM, and this is passive. There is no power to this. It's just little pieces of glass that combine the light into one stream and separate it back out into multiple streams. We can also do dense wave division multiplexing. Dense wave division multiplexing or DWDM, that is going to be a powered system. We can fit a lot more wavelengths of light on this, so we can get a higher band width. It can also go longer distances. With the powered version, we have a lot more options to send a lot more data over the same link than we do with course wave. However, you're going to see course wave used in as many applications as possible because it is not powered, and that makes it very easy to use in many different situations. To wrap up this physical layer technologies conversation, we have talked about a lot of detailed stuff. We started with the OSI model review and made sure we were looking at just the physical layer. We talked about the different mediums we can use, including copper, fiber optics, and electromagnetic spectrum with wireless. We talked about copper cabling, we talked about fiber optics and all the details of each of those, as well as the Ethernet designations for copper using twisted pair and for fiber optics using Ethernet up at layer 2. We're going to move on next and talk about Ethernet at layer 2 so we can continue this progression about talking about enterprise network infrastructure.

## Chapter 5 Ethernet Fundamentals

We're now going to focus on Ethernet terms and concepts. There is a tremendous amount of information to talk about Ethernet, so now we are going to focus on Ethernet. We're going to start with terms and concepts. Our goals for this module are first going to be to look at what CSMA/CD is, which is a very historic perspective of how Ethernet operates. We'll then talk about collision domains. We're going to talk about duplex and speed of Ethernet. Then we'll talk about the Ethernet frame. These are all very important concepts about Ethernet, so let's get started. Previously, we talked about the physical layer and, most specifically, the types of cables, both copper and fiber optics, that we need for Ethernet to work. Now we're going to talk about the data link layer protocol, Ethernet itself. The data link layer is responsible for moving data from one device to another device successfully. Sometimes we go to routers, and the router is going to take that message out of our layer 2 information and put it in new layer 2 information. Most of the internet and business networks and home networks all make use extensively of Ethernet of some kind. So you likely have seen Ethernet in your home with some device similar to this.

This is a cable modem router with a built-in wireless access point and layer 2 switch, all built into one device. This is an Ethernet device. If you look at the back of it, you'll see Ethernet jacks along with, in this image, you can see some cables here. You can actually see the EIA/TIA 568-B specification in that cable that's shown laying on the table.

This is the switch on the back of that wireless router. This switch here, this is a catalyst switch from Cisco. You might see this in an enterprise business.

This is a 48-port switch, much larger than you'd have in your home. It even has four SFP slots over on the right. What we can do is plug in an SFP or a laser there to give fiber optic communication to the switch. Those are for small form pluggables where we could plug in some optics for fiber optic communication to this switch. Here's a data center or a network closet someplace where here we're using an HP switch to connect together a bunch of devices.

Here you can see how we have the patch panel set up, and we're connecting our devices from our patch panel down to that layer 2 switch at the bottom of the rack. So these are instances where you're going to see Ethernet. It's going to be very much the same as your home connection. However, it's just going to be bigger when we use it in businesses.

# Chapter 6 CSMA/CD

CSMA/CD is carrier sense multiple access with collision detection. Legitimately, we don't really talk about or use this today when we work with Ethernet. The reason is that this is archaic technology. This is the original Ethernet that was originally made for industry back in 1982. Ethernet itself has origins that date very far back, probably farther back than almost any other technology that we still use today. Ethernet was developed in the late '60s, early '70s by a gentleman named Robert Metcalfe who did this as a project for graduate studies. It was his final project for his doctorate when he was studying engineering, and he made Ethernet or something like Ethernet is today. Then in '82, several engineers got together and they wrote the official specification for Ethernet, which was then published by IEEE as a specification that you can purchase for relatively inexpensively. CSMA/CD though, the original Ethernet, the way it worked is we had a coax cable, a very thick, solid core coax cable. Our networked devices would attach to this cable, and they would all share the same exact cable. In order for this to work, what would have to happen is each device on this cable would have to listen to the cable, make sure no one else was talking. Then when no one else was talking, then it would send data onto that wire. The data that it sent onto the wire was in the form of some voltage, specifically +5 volts. We would send this 5-volt signal out onto the wire. Then every device on this network segment would receive that signal. The idea here with carrier sense multiple access is that multiple devices are using the same cable. In order to pass messages on that cable, each device would listen for a break in the communication to find out when they could put signal onto the wire. When they were done transmitting, they would stop sending traffic, and then another device would keep listening to the wire for that break and then send traffic onto the wire to pass its information. If for whatever reason, two devices happen to simultaneously listen to the wire, hear that no one is talking and then start sending data onto the wire, well then both devices would be sending 5 volts onto that wire. That would create a 10-volt spike of voltage, and that is a collision. Each device then would detect that a collision occurred. The devices sending traffic onto the network would wait a random period of time, then listen to the wire again, see if anybody was talking, and then retransmit that data. So +10 volts is a voltage spike here, and the voltage spike is literally a collision. Carrier sense multiple access, we have lots of devices listening to one wire waiting for an opportunity to talk. If two devices happened accidentally talk at the same time, that's okay. That was intended. We have mechanisms then to detect that voltage spike or collision and then retransmit the data as necessary. This creates something called a collision domain, and it's a group of network devices that will simultaneously detect a voltage spike. In modern networks, we don't actually use this. In modern networks, we use something different, and I'll show you why. But does CSMA/CD still exist? Yes. Are our devices listening to the wire waiting for an open opportunity to talk? Yes. Do we ever have collisions in modern networks? Typically no, unless there's something broken.

## Chapter 7 Duplex and Speed

This will answer the question for us in a little bit of why CSMA/CD doesn't describe Ethernet the way it once did. So duplex and speed in Ethernet, we have two options here. The first one in the original Ethernet specification, all operated at half duplex. I can send information from the top PC to the bottom PC, or I can send information from the bottom PC to the top PC, but never at the same time. One device communicates at a time. This is a lot like a walkie-talkie. If I'm using a walkie-talkie, I push the button on the walkie-talkie, and when I'm pushing the button, I can't hear anything coming in, and I can talk then into the walkie-talkie and anybody listening on that channel can hear me, they just can't talk back to me until I'm done. Once I'm done, I release the button on the walkie-talkie, and somebody else can then press the button and communicate back to me. But we can only do that one at a time. This is in contrast to full-duplex communication, where both devices can send messages to each other simultaneously. They communicate at the same exact time, without worrying about collisions, and this is much more like the telephone. If I'm talking to my friend on the telephone, I can talk to my friend at the same time he or she is talking back to me, and we can talk over each other this way. Usually we're not doing this, we're waiting for each other's turns, but in a telephone conversation, sometimes we can send a message while the other person is talking to acknowledge that we heard what they're saying. We do that by saying uh-huh, oh yeah, oh that's exciting. The other person doesn't have to stop talking while we're doing that, we're just sending acknowledgment messages saying yeah, I heard you, keep going. Full-duplex communication Ethernet means that both devices can communicate at the same time. When we look at this in a modern sense, when we connect our device to a switch, when we communicate with a switch, we can either send traffic from the switch to the device, this is half duplex, or we can send traffic from the device to the switch. In this case, the only time we're going to have a collision is if the switch and the PC send information at the same time. This can happen if the cable is too long in half-duplex communication, and maybe the PC listens to the wire, sees that there's no one talking, starts sending data, the switch does the same thing at the same time, and they both send data at the same time, and there's a collision, a voltage spike. This can happen if we're using half-duplex communication. But when there's full-duplex communication, we have two channels open here. We can send and receive data simultaneously, there's no possibility that these two are going to have a collision because we have two channels to communicate, one descend to the switch, one descend from the switch to the PC, so we're not actually going to have a collision between our PC and the switch. There's even a bigger reason for this, and it has to do with our Ethernet speed/name designations. For Ethernet, that's always 10 Mbps. Fast Ethernet always means 100 Mbps, Gigabit Ethernet: 1 Gbps, 10 Gigabit Ethernet: 10 Gbps, and 40 Gigabit Ethernet: 40 Gbps. I refer to Ethernet pretty broadly, and other engineers are going to refer to this very broadly as well, and just know that if somebody uses the term Fast Ethernet, they're specifically saying 100 Mbps Ethernet. Fast Ethernet in modern networks is not very fast, but at the time it came out it was fast. It was 10 times faster than Ethernet. Typically, we're just using Ethernet as a broad term, and if we say Gig Ethernet or Gigabit Ethernet, we're specifically meaning 1Gbps Ethernet. In order to get speeds of gigabit, 10 Gb, and 40 Gb, we must use full duplex, we do not have a half duplex option for these. They must use full duplex. When we talk about collisions in modern networks, is it possible to have a collision on a gigabit Ethernet connection? Likely no. So does CSMA/CD apply here? Yes. The switch and the PC are still listening to the wire, making sure that the communication channel is open before they send data, but it's likely that the communication channel is always going to be open in the direction that they're sending it. In modern networks, we don't worry too much about collisions happening because we're operating at full-duplex communication.

## Chapter 8 Ethernet Frame Fundamentals

The Ethernet frame is the packaging on our data that we're sending. We package up our data in a frame so we can send it across the network, and the frame is going to be specific to Ethernet so that the Ethernet devices on our network can read it and process it and decide what to do with it, so the information contained in the frame is going to allow us to do that. This frame is going to contain a chunk of data, that's the gray part labeled Packet with a data link layer header. Our data link layer header here, that's our Ethernet header, that's going to be the Destination MAC Address, Source MAC Address, and Type. Then it's also going to have a footer, and it's going to have the FCS, or the frame check sequence. Our data here is the payload, that's the information that the frame is carrying. Typically that's a packet, which is a Layer 3 message. Sometimes it can be some Layer 2 messages, which aren't a packet at all, because they're not Layer 3. Layer 3 information is a packet. Layer 2 information is a frame. Let's look at the components here individually. First we'll start with the MAC addresses, the source and destination MAC addresses. Those are going to be composed of two different components, a Manufacturer ID and a Serial Number. They are 48 bits long, or 12 hexadecimal values, and the way this works is that the IEEE is the source of manufacturer IDs for MAC addresses. If you are a manufacturer of network interface cards, you can apply to IEEE to get the Ethernet specification and a manufacturer ID that you can use in order to make network interface cards. The network interface cards when they are produced, they are encoded directly with a hardware address that is supposed to be unique in the world. Sometimes we get duplicate MAC addresses, which cause problems, but it's pretty rare. We get the manufacturer ID from IEEE, which is Institute of Electrical and Electronics Engineers, and then we use that to create our network interface cards and the MAC addresses. We do that by then generating a serial number to go along with our manufacturer ID, we combine those together, and we get this 12 hexadecimal value MAC address. We can look up the manufacturer ID on the Internet and find out who made a certain network interface card. That gives us an idea of the types of devices that are sending data. The MAC address is an address that is burned onto the network interface card. We can change it in software, but that MAC address is part of the network interface hardware itself by design. The next component here is the type field. The type field is going to indicate what type of data is being moved here or at least what protocol is being used to carry the data that's in the message. If it's an IP packet, it's going to have a certain type code; if it's an IP version 6 packet, it's going to have a certain type code; if it's an ARP message, it's going to have a certain type code. That type code is there to indicate to the network interface card and the operating system that's running on our device what type of message is about to come and which software system to pass it into. If it's an IP version 4 message in our data, it'll have a certain type, and then our workstation will know to send that particular message the data in our payload. It'll send that to a certain part of the software based on that type field. The last field on here is the frame check sequence, and this contains something called a Cyclical Redundancy Check, or CRC. A CRC is an algorithm, and what we do is we take the entire frame with the Destination MAC Source, MAC Type, and the Data, and we run it through this algorithm and it generates a 32-bit number. So the sending device will run this through its calculations, it will populate the FCS field with that number it generates, and then it sends the frame out onto the wire. When the receiving device gets this frame, it's going to look at that FCS value, do its own calculation just like the sending device did, and it's going to compare the two values. If the value in the frame is the same one as the receiving device calculated, we got a good frame, we're going to process it. If they're different, well, then we throw the frame away and we hope that another protocol will resend that frame at another time. There is no mechanism in Ethernet to resend frames. We have to rely on other protocols, like TCP up at the transport layer, in order to make sure all those messages are sent and received correctly. But at Ethernet at Layer 2, we have no mechanism to determine whether a frame was successfully received or not. And that's okay, this whole system is designed to work together in order to achieve the end result. So the CRC is just validating that the frame sent is the same as the frame received. When we look at our payload or the stuff we're carrying in our frame, there is by default a maximum transmission unit size, and that is 1500 bytes of data can be carried by the frame, so that is our MTU, our maximum transmission unit. We can actually increase that if we need to. In most networks we're not going to do that, however, in data centers, specifically when we're working with storage area networks, we may want to increase that to make the hardware work more efficiently. Inside of data centers we might increase this to beyond 1500 bytes, and that would be a jumbo frame, but if our switches and our other devices don't support jumbo frames, they will actually just throw them away or it'll cause an error and we won't process them. But if we have the capabilities to turn on jumbo frames, we may want to do that in a data center so that we can have a more efficient and faster operation of some of our hardware. The entire frame with the data itself that's included, this is called a protocol data unit, or a PDU. You may hear this used in documentation and in instruction manuals that are more engineering related, but in day-to-day speak with other engineers, you will almost never talk about a protocol data unit, you will likely call it a frame instead, because it's just, that's what it is, but in engineering manuals and other documentation, you may hear this called a protocol data unit. In summary we talked about CSMA/CD and saw that it was a legacy operation of Ethernet. We looked at collision domains. We look at speed and duplex and saw how using full duplex communication resulted in less collisions or no collisions. Then, we took a look at the Ethernet frame, and understanding the Ethernet frame is going to be very important to understand what happens when we're going to talk about how Ethernet switches operate.

## Chapter 9 Ethernet Layer 2 Operation

First, we're going to talk about switch operation and what's special about it and how it works. Then we're going to talk about spanning tree protocol, which is a necessary protocol at layer 2 to prevent switches from stopping working. Then we're going to talk about VLANs and how important these virtual LANs are or VLANs are. Then we're going to follow up and talk about Power over Ethernet and its value and some of the details of the specification. The layer 2 switch is a very common feature in Ethernet networks. In fact, it's the thing that makes Ethernet work. The important part about the Ethernet switch is the MAC address table. It is the one table on a switch that tells us everything the switch needs to know in order to do its job. Here's how that works. The MAC address table is nothing more than a list of port numbers along with the MAC address of each device connected to that port. If we have a switch with six ports on it, we'll populate our MAC address table with each of the port numbers. How the MAC address table gets populated is inside of the switch on each one of the switch ports, there is something called an ASIC, or an application-specific integrated circuit. It's nothing more than a little chip, and all that chip is programmed to do is to read the destination and the source MAC addresses of our frames. If my device is sending a message into the switch, what'll happen is the switch will receive that message. It will read the frame header, grab the source MAC address, and then populate the

MAC address table. When all the devices do this, they will populate the MAC address table accordingly. Devices on a network, on an Ethernet network, they're pretty much constantly sending out traffic to the switch. It might be just bogus traffic. It could be some traffic like ARP where it's trying to find the MAC address of other devices. It could be just other traffic from the operating system trying to figure out what's on the network. Our devices are always sending traffic out typically, and the switch can read all those to populate the MAC address table pretty quickly. Then, when one of these devices wants to send a message to a device, when it sends that message into the switch, the ASIC reads the destination MAC address and then it consults the MAC address table and it says where is the device. Now what'll happen is the switch will build a small circuit in between these ports and send the message to the device. If there's more than one message, that switch circuit will remain in place to send all the messages from one device to the other device. Once that's done being transferred, that circuit will be torn down so it can be reused for other things. We build our circuit and then send our message up to the device. Many devices can communicate with each other at the same time without impacting each other's conversations. So the switch is a very efficient method of passing traffic between devices on a network. This is basically how Ethernet works. Using the MAC address table, we're able to find devices on the switch and forward the messages accordingly. Broadcast we've talked about already when we talked about IP addresses at layer 3, and there is a broadcast address in IP addresses. However, that is not what we're talking about here. As a matter of fact, broadcast IP addresses are not used very often at all. They were intended to have a purpose, but they really just aren't used very much. At layer 2, broadcasts are used constantly, and this is how the broadcasts work. If we take a look at our Ethernet frame again, the destination MAC address field, if that is all Fs or all binary 1s, what that means is that means this message is destined for every device connected to the layer 2 network.

| Destination MAC Address | Source MAC Address | Type | Data (Packet) | FCS |
|---|---|---|---|---|
| FFFFFFFFFFFF | 48 bits | 16 bits | MAX 1500 Bytes | 32 bits |

This is a layer 2 broadcast address of all Fs in the destination MAC address field. When the destination MAC address of the frame is all Fs, the frame is sent out all active interfaces on the switch except for the interface that received the message. When the switch receives the frame with a destination MAC address of all Fs, that frame is forwarded out all of the other interfaces, except the one that it was received on. A broadcast domain then is a group of network devices, which will receive a layer 2 broadcast message.

## Chapter 10 Spanning Tree Protocol

Switches are kind of neat because we can daisy chain them together, or we can put them in a loop, and what that means is we're just going to have one switch connected to another switch with an Ethernet cable, and this is going to make the switch work just fine. When we look at broadcast messages when we connect switches together, this is kind of what we have to take a look at. Sometimes devices don't know about other devices on the network, and we can send a broadcast message to learn about them. This is true, regardless of which device is sending it. However, this can become problematic, if we connect two switches together with two links. If we connect two switches together with two links, and we're not using any additional protocols, what can happen is if device A sends out a broadcast message, that broadcast message is then going to be sent out all active interfaces, which means we send the messages to all PCs on both interfaces. Both interfaces on the switch receive that broadcast message and then send it out all active interfaces, including back to the switch that sent it originally. Then this process is going to happen again when it gets to the top switch; it's going to send that broadcast message out all active interfaces, send the messages back out the opposite interface down to the bottom switch, and now we have this loop. Now we have a loop where broadcast messages are permanently being sent in this network. They will never, ever, ever stop, and devices will continuously broadcast. The devices aren't going to stop broadcasting messages; they're going to keep broadcasting more messages. This is starting to get very clogged up. What will happen eventually, once all the devices are sending messages and we have too many broadcasts in the system, it's going to clog up all the links, and it's going to overwhelm the switch, shut it down, and it's creating something called a broadcast storm, and we have to prevent this in Ethernet, or our networks just won't work anymore. It's very easy to accidentally connect two switches together, and the way we solve the broadcast storm is we shut down one of the ports. What we hoped to achieve by connecting the two switches together with two links to create some more bandwidth, actually doesn't do what we want it to do, and we end up having to implement something called Spanning Tree Protocol or STP, and Spanning Tree Protocol will actually just shut down one of the links and prevent it from being used at all. That way, when a broadcast message comes into the switch, it never gets repeated out the interfaces and sent back to the switch that sent it. This is going to prevent the broadcast storm. If for some reason, one of the links goes bad and gets disconnected, Spanning Tree Protocol will kick in. It will unblock the link, and it allow the traffic to flow. We do get some redundancy with this, but we don't double the bandwidth of our link. We need a different protocol to do that. Spanning Tree Protocol is going to work, no matter how many switches we have, or almost no matter how many switches we have here. If we have three switches connected together, the job of Spanning Tree Protocol is to figure out which port to block. We're only going to block one of these ports and we need to figure out which one to block, and that's the job of Spanning Tree Protocol.

# Chapter 11 VLANs and Port Aggregation

Next, let's take a look at port aggregation, which is something that, you know, we're going to solve the problem of spanning tree, we want some extra bandwidth, maybe, between these two switches, so we want definitely to have two links connecting the two switches, but we need a special protocol to do that, and that's where something called port aggregation comes in. Port aggregation is also called a port channel, an ether channel, a channel group; there's lots of different names for it, but it all has one thing in common, and that is that we're taking two or more links between two switches and we're bonding them together to behave as if they were one single link. That way we get extra bandwidth, we get some redundancy as well. The protocol we use to do that is called LACP, or Link Aggregation Control Protocol. This is the open source version of this and you'll oftentimes see it used when we're doing port aggregation or ether channel in a network. Let's move on to talk about VLANs. VLANs, if I had to characterize something in data networking that is one of the most important topics, VLANs would be it. If one can understand VLANs and IP addresses really well, you can understand almost anything in data networking and you can have a really good career in troubleshooting and supporting data networks in any enterprise. Remember I talked about a broadcast domain? If I send a message out with all Fs as the destination Mac address from a device, the switch repeats that information out to all the devices on that switch except for the port that it sent in. If we have two switches, I have two broadcast domains.

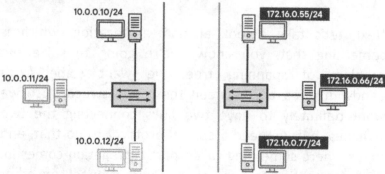

Over on the left-hand side, I have network 10.0.0.0/24, over on the right, I have network 172.16.0.0/24. These are two separate broadcast domains, and when I send messages into the switch, they just are repeated out to the other devices connected to their individual switch. If I label the network on the left, 1, and I label the network on the right, 2, and then I join them together with one switch, what I can do here is I can actually assign each of the ports to be on a specific VLAN.

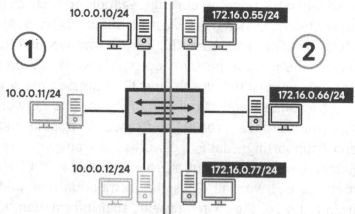

When I do that, if I assign the ports on the network 1 to be on VLAN 1, and I assign the ports on network 2 to be on VLAN 2, now when I send broadcast messages out from one of those devices, they only stay within their network. We only have one switch here, what we've told the switch here is to say, just send the broadcast message to only devices that are on the same VLAN as the interface you received it on; so VLAN 1 on the left, VLAN 2 on the right. This is really the basics of VLANs, this is all it is. What a VLAN is, it's a broadcast domain. What we're doing is we're creating a little mini switch within the switch, so we only forward traffic to the intended devices. This is wildly popular in data networks especially in enterprise businesses, but now in modern networks, when I have VLANs, oftentimes I have more than one switch that I'm using, and not all the devices that I'm using are on the same VLAN and on the same switch. So, let's mix this up. We have two networks, two VLANs, we're going to connect two switches together, so I've assigned the VLANs to each device, but now let's mix it up a little bit. We're going to put some of VLAN 2 on the switch on the left, some of VLAN 1 on the switch on the right, and now we still have the broadcast domain maintained, because the link that connects the two switches together is going to be a special kind of link that's going to be a trunk link, and the trunk link, its intended purpose is to carry more than one VLAN of information, but keep the VLANs separate yet.

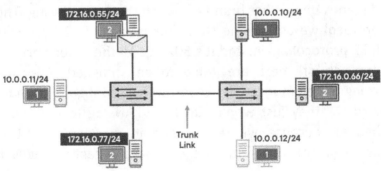

Now when I send a message from VLAN 2, so the device in the upper left there, if I send a message out to the switch, the switch is going to forward that message across to the other switch, but it's going to do something called tagging it. It adds another field into the frame header that says, this is on VLAN 2. It sends that message, that frame, across to the other switch, the other switch observes the VLAN tag, says this is for VLAN 2 device, removes the tag from the frame header, then it forwards the message onto the other device on VLAN 2. This way we keep our traffic separate. If there's a broadcast message that happens, we're only sending it to devices that have the same exact VLAN number. The same thing is happening if we send a message from VLAN 1. When you send it from VLAN 1, that's going to have a VLAN tag added to the frame header, that VLAN tag will maintain itself on the frame header while it traverses the trunk link, the other switch will observe that this frame is for VLAN 1, it will remove the tag and then forward the frame onto the device. VLANs are really just creating mini networks that we separate using VLAN tags in the frame as their traversing a trunk link to talk between two devices. These are often called tagged ports on a trunk link. These ports can be configured as trunk, they might be configured as tagged, it depends upon what brand of switch that you're using. This protocol we use on the trunk link is called 802.1q. It's an IEEE protocol again, and it's 802.1q. All the other ports on our network here are going to be untagged. They are going to be untagged; however, we will configure them for a VLAN, they just won't add the VLAN tag to the frame header, because we don't need it, we don't want it, actually. The only time we can have a tagged VLAN is when we are communicating between two interfaces that support the 802.1q protocol, and typically, our PCs at the end here, we don't need that, because we're just sending traffic to the switch, we don't need to use 802.1q, we're just sending traffic to the switch, the switch can see what VLAN it's on based on the port's configuration. This network that I have set up here with the VLANs on it, this is a very common setup for networks with VLANs; however, a more common one that you're going to see, especially at a users desktop in a modern network is going to be where they have a VoIP phone on their desk. The VoIP phone is typically going to have a small switch in the back of it, so what we're going to do is we're going to run a cable from the switch to the phone, and then we have another cable that we run from the phone to our PC, and what'll happen here is the phone to the PC is going to be untagged and that's going to be on some kind of data VLAN, and then the phone is going to be on its own separate VLAN, a voice VLAN, and that's going to be connected via a trunk link up to the switch.

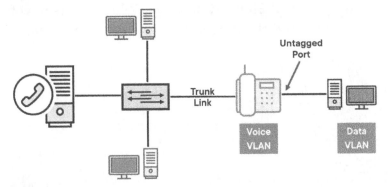

When we do this, we have separate traffic then for our phone versus our computer, and the intention here is that when we're talking on the telephone, we want a very high quality signal, we want our voice to come through loud and clear to the person we're talking to, we want to be able to hear the person we're talking to loud and clear, and by separating our traffic from our PC, from the phone, what that allows us to do is it allows us to give priority on the network to our voice calls versus our data network, which can tolerate a lot more latency. We can have a lot more delay, when we are just surfing the web or sending an email, we can handle a 50 to 100 millisecond or 500 millisecond delay, where a voice conversation can't handle that. We'll give priority to our voice traffic by having two separate VLANs at our desk; one for the phone traffic, one for the PC's traffic and there'll be a trunk link where we tag each traffic individually going into the switch. In summary we've talked about Ethernet and switch operation. We talked about spanning tree protocol and took a look at how the spanning tree protocol blocks ports. We looked at VLANs and we looked at Power over Ethernet. I hope you have a much better understanding of how Ethernet works now. We're going to go on and use our knowledge of Ethernet and layer 2 broadcasts now to understand more about how layer 3 works with routing.

## Chapter 12 How to Route IP Traffic

Our goals are to do a very brief review of the OSI model again, so we can stay focused on what layer of the OSI model we're talking about for different protocols and different components and networking. We're going to introduce network layer communication so we can see what's happening at layer 3 when we're using IP to send traffic between one device and another. To do that, we're going to need ARP, or Address Resolution Protocol, so we'll explain that in detail. ARP is a layer 2 protocol that works directly in conjunction with layer 3 and Internet Protocol or IP. We're then going to describe the purpose and the use of the default gateway to route traffic between unique layer 3 networks. We're going to describe how IP routing works and how to build routing tables on routers, and last, we'll cover Traceroute. Traceroute is a nifty utility that can show us all of the routers that exist between my workstation and some device out on the network or on the internet. When we're looking at the OSI model and we're talking about routing IP traffic, we're going to make use of the bottom three layers, the physical layer, the data link layer, and the network layer. The protocols that are going to be interacting together are going to be some layer 2 protocols and some layer 3 protocols. The reason for this is that at the data link layer, that's responsible for moving traffic from one device to another device in small increments. In order to get from my workstation over to the server, I have to go through lots of little increments of networks that are mostly Ethernet, but some are different. If you remember,

Ethernet is a layer 2 network. We put our information inside of a frame, and then we forward that frame onto a switch, and the switch is able to create a connection inside the switch between one device and another. Layer 2 is critical for passing traffic between our devices. However, in order to get traffic from one device on the internet to the other device from our client to our server, we need to make use of all those individual little data link layer connections, but we also need some map, some bigger picture utility that's going to allow us to get across the entire internet efficiently, and that's where the network layer comes in with Internet Protocol. So here we're going to use routers in order to move our traffic from one segment of the network to another. The path between our workstation and our server is going to be full of routers. This is going to be interacting directly with layer 2, because here is the device on our network. This is our cable modem for our internet service in our home. This is a layer 2 bridge, and all it does is it converts Ethernet frames into DOCSIS frames. It takes the packet out of the Ethernet frame and puts it into a DOCSIS frame. DOCSIS is the protocol that cable modems use in order to communicate between the cable modem and the internet service provider. We're just going to pull the packet out of the frame and put it into a new frame; that's all this layer 2 bridge does. All these devices are very critical in our network, because they're going to help us move the traffic from one end of the internet to the other. The internet itself is full of routers, and we're going to use Traceroute to see all the routers between our workstation and a server that we try to reach.

## Chapter 13 Address Resolution Protocol

Let's keep this simple and start looking at a basic network. I have a very simple network. I have two devices, 10.0.0.10 and 10.0.0.20, and they're connected to a router, and that router is connected to the internet. When I am on my local workstation, whenever I'm working there, it's going to be sending traffic locally, so between 10.0.0.10 and 10.0.0.20, in my router.

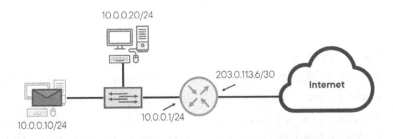

It's also going to be communicating with the internet or at least attempting to communicate with the internet. When I'm looking at this, there's going to be two different modes that I'm operating. One, I'm going to have to use the router to forward the traffic. The other one, I'm just communicating locally between two devices. So let's take a look at all the components that make this kind of communication work. We're going to start by looking at just a conversation between our two internal devices here, 10.0.0.10 and 10.0.0.20. We're going to start with the IP packet. When we try to send a ping message, which is what we're going to try to do here, we're going to ping from 10.0.0.10 to 10.0.0.20, we're going to be using the ICMP protocol, or Internet Control Message Protocol. That protocol is what ping uses to send the message and get a response. That ICMP data is put inside of an IP packet, which is composed of a source IP address, a destination IP address, a time to live, as well as quite a bit of other information in order to properly pass that packet.

| Source IP Address | Destination IP Address | TTL | Other | ICMP |
|---|---|---|---|---|

I'm leaving the other information as just other because it's not critical to understand how this process works. The other information is going to be critical when you do deeper dives into internet protocol and see how it works. This IP packet, then is going to be put inside of a Layer 2 frame, and the Layer 2 frame is going to change often as it moves across the network. The Layer 2 frame, we've looked at this before, it has a destination MAC address, followed by a source MAC address, and then the Layer 3 protocol that it's carrying, which in this case, is IP version 4. We put all that inside of our message here, and that message can go, then onto the workstation and get sent between our two devices. So let's look at the detailed process of how this happens. We start with ICMP on 10.0.0.10. I'm going to type in ping 10.0.0.20. That's going to allow us to generate an IP packet header and fill in our source and destination IP addresses. Additionally, we're going to fill in the time to live value here, which is going to be 128. That value is set by the operating system, and it can range between 1 and 255. Most operating systems defaulted to 128. What that value does for us is it's a counter. Every time that packet goes through a router, that TTL, or time to live, will be decreased by 1. That way, if we go through 128 routers, the packet says, yeah, that's too far away from me. I'm just going to throw it away. It's just not worth it anymore. What this really does is it helps

186

routers who may have accidentally configured themselves in a loop so that if it gets into that loop, the packets won't live there forever, and they'll eventually just die out. The time to live value, we're going to see what happens with that later on when we look at sending a message on the other side of the router. For now, we're just communicating within our own local Ethernet segment here. Once we have this generated, we can then put this message in a frame. We put the packet inside of our frame. We fill in our source MAC address, which is the MAC address of our workstation. Our Layer 3 protocol is IPv4. We need to know our destination MAC address, which is the MAC address of 10.0.0.20. The problem here is I don't know what that MAC address is. My workstation doesn't either. So we have to figure out what that is. That's where ARP comes in. Address Resolution Protocol is going to come in and save the day. Here's how ARP works. We've built most of it. We just need to know the destination MAC address. Before we can fill in that, we need to create another frame here. And this time, we're going to say, hey, who has 10.0.0.20? This is an ARP request saying, hey, 10.0.0.20, if you're out there, send me your MAC address. That's going to go right inside of a frame header. We can fill in our source MAC address because we know that. We can fill in our Layer 3 protocol. In this case, it's not actually a Layer 3 protocol. ARP is a Layer 2 protocol. We don't actually have Layer 3 here, but we're going to tell the frame header which protocol is being carried in the data section. Then for our destination MAC address, I'm going to put all Fs in here because I want every single device on the Layer 2 network to receive this message and be able to answer the question, who has

10.0.0.20? If the device doesn't have it, it can throw this message away. If the device does have the MAC address for 10.0.0.20, it'll respond. We put that frame inside of our message. We send it out onto the network. It goes out to all the devices except the sending device. The device that has 10.0.0.20 says, I have this MAC address because it's me. I know what that is. So, we hang on to our source MAC address from 10.0.0.10. We then create a response to our ARP request. And we say, yep, here we go. Here is the MAC address for 10.0.0.20. We fill in our destination MAC address because we know who sent it to us. We fill in our source MAC address because we know what our own MAC address is there on 10.0.0.20. We then send that on the wire over to 10.0.0.10. 10.0.0.10 then pulls that frame out, looks at the ARP reply, says, okay, the destination MAC address is right here. I can take my ping message that I wanted to send before, fill in the destination MAC address, put that out onto the wire, and say ping 10.0.0.20, and now I'm able to forward that message directly onto that device. You might say, but why don't we just send it to the broadcast address? The reason is that would get messy. That would defeat the purpose of the switch. It means all the traffic we'd send out would all go to all the devices. Now our switch could easily get overwhelmed with traffic, and it would really defeat all of the efficiency we have built into it. ARP really saves the day. Additionally, ARP is going to maintain something called an ARP cache or an ARP table. That ARP table is going to be a mapping of a Layer 3 IP address to a Layer 2 MAC address. My workstation will maintain this ARP cache and the next time we need to send a message to 10.0.0.20, we're not going to have to send an ARP message out again. We can just look in our ARP table and see that we already have that information without having to ask for it. That ARP cache is only valid for a few minutes or maybe even only 90 seconds, depending upon the operating system. After that time, the ARP entry will be removed, and the workstation will have to resend an ARP message out to get the updated Mac entry. That's allowing for devices to change their IP addresses on the network because when you change the IP address, it's going to be associated with a new MAC address, and ARP will have to figure out what that is. Something to note here is that we have looked at MAC address tables on switches. The MAC address table on a switch takes a Layer 1 interface, a physical port that we're plugging a cable into, and it maps that physical port to a Layer 2 address or a MAC address. The ARP table is located on devices that have Layer 3 capabilities and is going to map a Layer 3 address, a Layer 3 IP address, to a Layer 2 MAC address. These two tables have very specific purposes. They are not the same as each other. When I teach students this, oftentimes this gets confusing because we're looking at MAC addresses. Sometimes we need to look at both the ARP table and the MAC address table, but just know they're not the same table.

## Chapter 14 How to Send Ping to Default Gateway

Let's continue about how IP routing works. We actually haven't even gotten to IP routing yet because the understanding of ARP is so important to understand how IP routing works. I've changed up my network a little bit here, and instead of having the internet on to the right-hand side, I have replaced that with another PC on the 192.168.10.8 network.

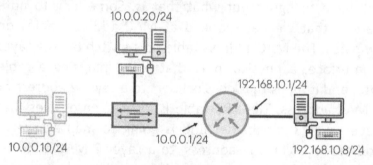

So let's take a look at how this works now when we try to send a message from 10.0.0.10 to 192.168.10.8. We're going to first build our packet, put our source and destination IP addresses in there, we're going to put that then inside of our frame, and we're going to start to build our frame. We know it, once again, our source MAC address. We don't know our destination MAC address yet, so we're going to have to find out what that is. Do we send an ARP request and say who has 192.168.10.8? We absolutely cannot do that. We cannot ARP for the destination IP address because it's not on our own local network. Remember, ARP messages cannot be sent through a router, so we're not going to be able to send the message out asking who has the

MAC address for 192.168.10.8. Instead, what we're going to do is we're going to consult our routing table on our PC. The routing table on our PC is going to know how to reach two things typically. It's going to know how to reach our local network, 10.0.0.0, and it's going to have a route for everything else, which is going to be our default gateway, or our default router. A gateway is a router. They're the same thing. So the default gateway is the default router and in this case, it's 10.0.0.1. When my PC is trying to send a message to an IP address that's not my local subnet, it will automatically look up the default gateway's IP address, and then we're going to do an ARP request for the default gateway, in this case, 10.0.0.1. We'll send out our message saying who has 10.0.0.1? It's a broadcast, so all the devices on the 10.0.0 network can get it. The router says, that's me, I have that MAC address. Let me build a message and send it back to you. Here's my MAC address. We can take our original message with our ping in it, going to 192.168.10.8. We can now fill in our destination MAC address of the router. In the beginning of this conversation about routing, I told you that we're sending messages from one device to another. Here we're sending it from the PC to the router, and our frame is what accomplishes that. We put in our source and destination MAC addresses of our frame. We then can put that out onto the wire because now we know the destination MAC address of our default gateway. That gets sent to the router. The router then opens up that message, says, hey this this message is for me. That's my destination MAC address. We throw the frame header away and we open up the packet. Once we're in the packet, we look at the destination IP address and say, do I know how to reach that? The way that the router does that is it looks inside of its routing table. So on the router, we can issue a command called show ip route, and that will show me the routing table that is for that router. This router knows about two different networks. It knows how to reach our source network of 10.0.0.0/24, that's connected to fa0/0. That's just the name of the interface that we send it out of. Then we have 192.168.10.0/24, and that's connected to interface fa0/1, a different physical interface on the router. What we do now is we take our destination IP address and we compare it to what the router knows how to reach. Here we look at is 192.168.10.8 on the 10.0.0.0 network. Nope, it's 192.168.10.8 on the 192.168.10.0/24 network. Yes, it is. And if you remember for IP addressing, one of them I had you do is determine the network associated with a specific host. Remember there's all 0s in the host portion of a network address, so all we're doing here is we're saying, with a /24 mask, 192.168.10.8 is on the 192.168.10.0 network.

```
Router# show ip route

Codes: C - Connected, S - Static


C  10.0.0.0/24 connected to F0/0
C  192.168.10.0/24 connected to F0/1
   192.168.10.8
```

That's connected to fa0/1. Now what we can do is we can start building our frame again. First though, before we do that, we have to decrease the Time-to-Live value because we've just processed it through a router. Our Time-to-Live is going to decrease by one. Now, we're going to start to construct our frame header. We know what the source MAC addresses, it's the source MAC address from F0/1. We don't know the destination MAC address, so we have to put that message in the queue for a second while we go use ARP to find out who has the MAC address for 192.168.10.8. We send that message out, F0/1. My device says, that's me, I have that MAC address. I put the MAC address in a message, and I send it back to the router. The router adds it to its ARP cache. We can fill in our destination MAC address and put this message out onto the wire, send it over to 192.168.10.8, and now 192.168.10.8 can reply to my ping. This is the very slow version of this process of my message, leaving 10.0.0.10, getting sent to the router through the frame. If you noticed, my IP packet was unaltered except for the Time-to-Live. I didn't mess around changing IP addresses, I let the frame figure out how to reach my router, then the router looked inside of my frame at the packet header to find out where it should send it. Once it found out where to send it, it constructed a new frame and forwarded that message on. The frames, when we're sending packets across the network, the frames are just little temporary vehicles for our packet to get moved from one router to the next.

## Chapter 15 How to Build Routing Tables

Whenever we have a network, usually we're going to have more than one router. As a matter of fact, the internet is full of routers. It's really what makes the internet work is all these routers. There's routers, and there's connections between the routers.

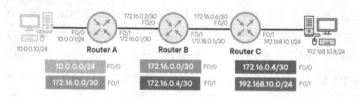

Here I have routers A, B, and C, and I have four unique networks. Connected to router A is 10.0.0.0/24, and then connected also to router A, the connection between router A and B is 172.16.0.0/30. Then I have 172.16.0.4/30, connecting routers B and C together. And then last, I have 192.168.10.0 connected to F0/1 of router C. So, by default, router A knows how to reach two networks, 10.0.0.0 and 172.16.0.0/30. And I've listed the interfaces that those are connected to right next to it. This is effectively what the routing table looks like. It's the networks that the router knows how to reach. Router B is going to know how to reach two networks, 172.16.0.0 and 172.16.0.4, both of those /30. And then last, router C knows how to reach 172.16.0.4/30 and 192.168.10.0/24. If I try to send a message though, so if I say on 10.0.0.10, let's ping 192.168.10.8, and I send that message out into the network, the first router receives that, and it looks up in the routing table, and it says, I don't know how to reach that at all. I have no route to that. What the router does is it throws the message away. It says I don't know how to reach it. I'm going to throw it away. Occasionally, the router will send a message back to the sending device saying, yeah, I don't know how to reach that. It all depends on if the router is configured to send an ICMP message back to the sending device saying, yeah, I don't know how to reach that. What do we need to do? We need to build the routing table. We're going to build this statically. We're going to manually configure each of the routes. The idea here that we want is that router A needs to know about all the networks that are not directly connected to it, as well as how to reach those. One of the networks that router A does not know how to reach is 172.16.0.4. Let's add that to the routing table and say we'll reach that by going to router B. We manually add the century in and say, hey, if I'm trying to reach this network, send it over to router B. And the next hop address that we would send that to is 172.16.0.2, which is router B's F0/0 interface. Then we need to know how to reach 192.168.10.0, and that also gets sent to router B. We can't send it to router C because we're not directly connected to that, but we can send it to router B because we are directly connected to it. Then we'll let router B figure out what to do with it. So we'll send our message, then onto router B. So now router B needs a complete routing table. It needs to know how to reach 10.0.0.0/24, which gets sent to router A, and it needs to know how to reach 192.168.10.0/24, and that gets sent to router C. Then last, router C needs to know how to reach two networks. It needs to know how to reach 10.0.0.0/24. We can send that traffic to router B, so router B can get it over to router A. Also, 172.16.0.0/30, which is also connected to router B. Now we have a complete routing table. When I try to send my message now to 192.168.10.8, it gets sent to my default gateway, which is router A. Router A looks up in its routing table and says, do I know how to reach this? It says, I send that message to router B, so it puts it inside of a frame, sends it over to router B. Router B looks up in its routing table. It says, hey, do I know how to reach this network? It says, yes I do. I send it over to router C, so we decrease the TTL by 1, put it in a new frame, send it over to router C. Router C then looks up in its table and says, hey, do I know how to reach 192.168.10.8? It says, yep, it's directly connected to my fast Ethernet 0/1 interface, and we can send the message directly to the device, then. Then, 192.168.10.8 can reply to the ping message, and we have a path all the way back. Router C needs to send this message to Router B. Router B needs to send this message to Router A. Router A is directly connected to the 10.0.0.0 network, so we can send it right onto the intended device.

This is the idea of IP routing. Every single router has a little map of how to reach all of the networks. As long as that map is maintained correctly and all the links are up, we can send traffic between our two devices. The internet is full of routers. When we are in an enterprise business or a large enterprise business, we have lots of routers there as well. It keeps all of our traffic separated and moving very efficiently. In order to get IP routing to work right, we need to have more sophisticated options than manually configuring them. Let's look at how we do that. IP routing can happen one of two ways. We've talked about static routing. That's where I manually enter in my routes. The trouble with static routing is that once I enter the route in, it's permanently in there, and it's unchanged unless I go manually change it in the future. Another option I have here is something called dynamic routing. Dynamic routing is going to use a routing protocol in order to build the routing tables themselves. There's several different protocols we can use here. One of them is RIP, or Routing Information Protocol. This is a very old one that's not used at all anymore. It's very slow, and it's not very good at its job. However, it was useful back in the 80s in early networks to dynamically build routing tables when we didn't need networks that were extremely resilient. Today though, we need a more resilient routing infrastructure in our networks, so we might use EIGRP. This is Cisco's routing protocol called Enhanced Interior Gateway Routing Protocol. It's available on Cisco devices. It is written as a publicly available protocol. Any company can implement this. However, EIGRP is, in some cases, kind of on its way out of being used. Other places, it's being used more. EIGRP may or may not be used very often in a network. I know that's a little odd to say. OSPF, though, Open Shortest Path First, this routing protocol is extremely popular in enterprise networks and networks of big businesses. There's one other routing protocol we need to mention here, and that's Border Gateway Protocol, or BGP. This routing protocol is used on the public internet in order to move routes between different businesses and internet service providers. BGP is kind of nifty because it's more like a scripting language with lots of parameters that we can configure. Those parameters allow us to implement contracts that two different internet service providers might agree to in order to figure out who pays for what traffic as it's moving across the internet. We categorize these routing protocols into different categories. The only time I've ever really used these categories is on an exam. I have really never talked about these categories when I am working with other engineers. I don't say, hey, we should use a distance vector routing protocol here. I've never said that ever. But I have taken many exams where it asks me which of these routing protocols are distance vector protocols. RIP and EIGRP are distance vector protocols. OSPF is a link state routing protocol. It pays attention to the different links and keeps a map of all the links so it can provide the best path through that network. BGP is kind of a hybrid. It makes use of lots of different parameters so that engineers and businesses can figure out the best path to allow two internet service providers or two businesses or a business and an ISP the best path to move traffic through a network. These top three are called interior gateway protocols. In fact, EIGRP has interior gateway protocol written right in it. These are meant for inside of a business. Then BGP is an exterior gateway protocol, meaning it's used to route traffic between different businesses or different ISPs. Each of these routing protocols is given an administrative distance. That way, if we have more than one routing protocol running on our system, our routers know which route to use in the routing table. The higher the number, the lower the priority of routing protocol. RIP is given the lowest priority. BGP is given the highest priority, and EIGRP and OSPF sit right in the middle. This is the route priority. It determines which route is the good one to add to the routing table. In summary we did a brief review of the OSI model, saw that we were going to be examining the connection between the data link layer and frames and the network layer and packets. We introduced network layer communication with IP packets. We explained how ARP worked and saw how necessary address resolution protocol is to build frames correctly to get those packets to route from the workstation to a router. We described the default gateway and saw how important that router is in our network. Then we described IP routing and took a look at different methods of constructing routing tables. I hope you found this really valuable. In data networking, this routing technology is some of the cooler stuff to get to work with. It's kind of like the plumbing of the internet. It's really what makes everything work and gets messages from one device to another, and understanding it gives you a leg up in almost every single technology that you'll work with in IT.

## Chapter 16 Wireless Networking Fundamentals

First, we are going to talk about the basics of wireless and discuss the physical layer components of wireless, including wireless channels. Then we're going to move up to the data link layer of wireless and talk about the 802.11 protocols that allow us to communicate with wireless, as well as the technologies involved in each of the 802.11 protocols. Then we're going to talk about encrypting wireless and how we secure wireless networks to prevent people from snooping in on our data. Last, we'll wrap up and talk about cellular wireless options specifically used for data networks. When we look at the OSI model and we talk about wireless networks, there are two components to it, just like we saw in other versions of Ethernet. We took a look at the physical layer components using copper cables and fiber optics. Then we took a look at how Ethernet operated at the data link layer. Well here, we're going to do the same thing. We're going to take a look at the physical layer components of wireless ethernet and then the data link layer components of wireless Ethernet. Let's check out the basic physics of wireless. This is the physical layer component of it. We've seen this electromagnetic spectrum before when we talked about fiber optics and using lasers to light up those fiber optics.

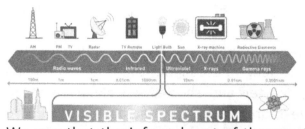

We saw that the infrared part of the spectrum is what we used here. The electromagnetic spectrum is made up of different wavelengths of photons traveling through space. Over on the far left, we have the very large wavelengths that includes AM and FM radio, TV. And then as we move closer to the visible light spectrum, we get radar, infrared, then visible light. Then as we move away from the visible light spectrum in the other direction, the wavelengths get smaller, and smaller, and smaller, and these wavelengths, then can get to the point where they can actually be dangerous to living creatures because the wavelengths are actually smaller than atoms, and they can actually knock apart atoms as those waves, like gamma rays, hit our bodies, and it can cause things like cancer. The electromagnetic spectrum here is consisted of basically waves of photons. There's a lot of physics involved in this. We're not going to go too deep into that though, but we do need to understand what a wavelength is. A wavelength is nothing more than in an electromagnetic wave or any wave, for that matter, we're measuring the distance between the peak of one wave and the peak of the next wave in the series. The wavelength is that distance that is directly related to frequency. Frequency is measured in hertz, or cycles per second. What we do here is we're measuring the peak of each wave as it passes across a fixed point. That is going to get us how many cycles per second that wave is moving, or it's our frequency. The shorter the wavelength, the higher the frequency. If we keep getting shorter and shorter wavelengths, we're going to have more waves hit that center line more often, which increases the frequency. Shorter wavelength, higher frequency. When we use the electromagnetic spectrum, we need to select a component of it that we can make use of and transmit a signal and receive a signal. To do that, we need something called a channel. A channel is a range of frequencies we can use to transmit information. A single frequency of the electromagnetic spectrum is not enough to transmit data because what we need to do is we need to modulate between a couple different frequencies in order to encode the data on the signal or on that electromagnetic wave. A channel is a range of frequencies we use to transmit information. When we're talking about wireless communication, the wireless communication that we're looking at here falls in this yellow bar on the electromagnetic spectrum. What we do is we select a range of frequencies there and divide it up into channels. Here is the 2.4 GHz Wi-Fi spectrum.

2.4 GHz is the frequency that we're using, and it's a frequency range between 2.4 GHz and 2.499 GHz. We divide that up into numerous channels. But in order to make use of it for 802.11 wireless, we need a 22 MHz channel in order to accomplish our goal of transmitting data. That 22 MHz channel, then composes itself of multiple individual channels. Each of these channels is about 5 MHz apart. When we're using wireless and the 2.4 GHz Wi-Fi spectrum, we can only use three different channels of the 13 or 14 channels, depending upon which country you're in, available to us. In this case, we use channel 1, 6, and 11, and those are the three channels we can use with 2.4 GHz wireless. Additionally, we have the 5 GHz wireless spectrum.

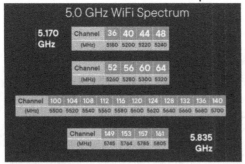

That spectrum ranges from 5.170 GHz all the way up to 5.835 GHz. These channels are 20 MHz apart. We have 36, 40, 44, 48, and so on that we can use here. However, the channels in the middle, channels 52 through 140 here, these require something special. If we are going to use these channels in an 802.11 wireless Ethernet network, we have to use something called DFS, or dynamic frequency selection. The reason for this is is these channels are also used by the military to do certain types of transactions, whatever those transactions might be. The military can use these for radar and other things. If we have an enterprise network environment and we're near an area where the military might use these, our equipment needs to detect that some external entity is using these channels. If they're using the channels, we need to automatically switch to one that isn't one of these channels. This is a regulatory impact of using 5.0 GHz Wi-Fi spectrum here. In our home networks, you typically will not see the 5 GHz Wi-Fi spectrum use these at all. It only is going to use 36, 40, 44, 48, and then 149, 153, 157, and 161, so only 8 channels available in our home networks. However, in enterprise networks, we can make use of these additional wireless channels, 4 to 5 GHz, because the systems we set up are capable of detecting the use of these channels and automatically switching to something different. Then for the physical layer of 802.11 wireless Ethernet, we have these two different spectrums of electromagnetic signals we can choose from in order to send and receive our data.

## Chapter 17 Wireless 802.11 Protocols

Wireless Ethernet protocols - the 802.11 protocol suite is the data link layer components of wireless Ethernet. Let's talk about a history of this. All these 802.11 protocols are part of the IEEE suite of protocols for wireless Ethernet. If you remember, I've talked about 802.something quite a bit; 802.something is referring to Ethernet. When we talked about trunk links, it was 802.1q. That was an Ethernet protocol specifically related to trunk links, 802.11 are the protocols related to wireless Ethernet. To start off, in 1997, that's when 802.11 was first specified as a wireless Ethernet protocol. This is a very early version. It was specific for enterprise business markets. There was no wireless encryption involved. It was very expensive and had a very limited use. By 1999, we solidified wireless Ethernet a little bit more into two markets now, the home market with 802.11b, that's the consumer market, and then the enterprise business market with 802.11a. We're going to talk about the differences between these two protocols in just a bit, but the idea here was is that these protocols were separated out so that industry could make use of one of them and consumer market would make use of a different one. The consumer market version was quickly found out to be too slow, so they enhanced it in 2003 with 802.11g, which gave it a little bit faster communication, a little bit more reliable system. Then by 2009, 802.11n was available, and 802.11n kind of converged the enterprise business market with the home network. It was still two systems; however, the protocol itself was used in both the consumer devices and the enterprise business devices. When I say enterprise, what I mean there is a big business, something that has 1000 users or 10,000 users or more in their networks. It's a very large business, and the data networks that are needed for that are a lot more sophisticated than your home network. By 2009, almost every laptop and wireless device that you purchased had WiFi built into it already. In 2003, that started to happen, but before 2003, typically you had to buy a separate wireless card for your devices in order to make them work correctly. By 2009, it made sense that the laptop that you used at work would need to support both the business wireless that's set up as well as the home wireless that's set up in order to have that be portable, and by 2009, smartphones were becoming very, very, very popular, and that protocol was built into all the smartphones. As time passed, 2013 came around, we came out with 802.11ac, and then in 2018, we enhanced it again with WiFi 6 with 802.11.ax. Let's go take a look at each one of these protocols individually now. Let's start with 802.11a; 802.11a used the 5.0 GHz spectrum only. It could transfer data up to 54Mbps, and it was initially for enterprise use only. You did not typically have 802.11a in your home networks. You would have to use 802.11b in your home networks. Then 802.11b is a 2.4 GHz spectrum only. It could transfer data up to 11Mbps, and it was initially for SOHO use only. SOHO is small office/home office use. Then 802.11g was in an enhancement to 802.11b, and again used only the 2.4 GHz spectrum. It could transfer data up to 54Mbps, which is much faster. It could compete with 802.11a now, and it could be used in both enterprise and small office/home office, although typically we were still seeing enterprises using 802.11a. At this point, if you had a laptop with a built-in wireless card that was supporting 802.11g, you could use it both at work and at home. Then 802.11n was a convergence of protocols for business and home use, and it could make use of both 2.4 and the 5.0 GHz spectrum. As wireless became more prolific, that 2.4 GHz spectrum became very heavily used, and if your neighbors were using it and you were using it, you could oftentimes get overlap of channels, and it made it more difficult to communicate at higher speeds. 802.11n offered us an opportunity to use both 2.4 and 5.0 GHz in order to increase our throughput on our wireless links, and we could transfer data at up to 300Mbps. We're moving up to do faster and faster wireless transmission. To accomplish this, it uses something called MIMO, or multiple input/multiple output. What MIMO is really just means we have multiple antennas that we're using, and we can send signals on one antenna and have it received by our wireless access point. We could send data on a separate antenna and have it received by our wireless access point. We could also communicate simultaneously with both antennas, and that would increase the amount of data we could transfer to our wireless access points. 802.11ac, that made use of the 5.0 GHz spectrum only. We were moving away from the 2.4 GHz spectrum with 802.11ac. This could transfer data up to 1.3Gbps, which is now a similar speed that we can get by having a wired connection. With wireless though, the throughput that we get is directly dependent upon lots of circumstances, including how far away from the access point we are? What is in the way between us and the access point? Are there walls? Are there trees? Is there water around? Is the building made of metal? Things like this. The speed is directly related to our location and the physics around there. 802.11ac that can make use of multi-user MIMO and beamforming. What multi-user MIMO is it means that we can allow more than one wireless client with multiple antennas the ability to use the same access point with multiple antennas at the same time. MIMO initially only worked with one user at a time. Multi-user MIMO allows for multiple users to do this at the same time. In addition, beamforming became a thing, and beamforming is a really nifty implementation of a wireless technology that allows us to direct a signal right at the client. We can use multiple antennas to triangulate and use some algorithms to figure out where in space the wireless client is, and then we can beam the signal directly to that client, and that allows us to have a very directed broadcast of the electromagnetic signal that allows us to send more data faster to that device. With 802.11ax, this is our modern standard here. This is WiFi 6. This can use 2.4 GHz, 5.0 GHz, plus the ISM bands, that is the industrial, scientific, and medical bands, which were typically reserved for research purposes. With 802.11ax, we have an opportunity to use more channels in order to get more throughput to our devices. This can make use of MIMO and multi-user MIMO and beamforming as well, as well as something called OFDMA. OFDMA stands for orthogonal frequency division multiple access. This really is a pretty sophisticated topic to understand. When we're talking about electromagnetic signals, there are multiple accesses that we can send the data on, and OFDMA makes use of sending as much data, packing as much information as we can, onto one wireless signal as possible. It allows us to really increase our reliability and our throughput to our devices using OFDMA.

## Chapter 18 Wireless Ethernet Operation

Let's talk about wireless Ethernet operation now and some of the terminology we need to understand in order to learn how wireless networks actually work. In our home or small business Wi-Fi network, a SOHO network, we're typically going to have just one access point or maybe two access points working as a pair with each other. That access point is going to send out a signal to wireless clients in our home. Those wireless clients might be a laptop. It might be a smartphone or a tablet or an IoT device, or Internet of Things device, like a smart lightbulb. It could be a smart outlet or some toy or other things in our network. The access point is the central hub. That's the device that's sending out the signal, and it's receiving the signal. Our wireless clients, like I said, this could be laptops, smartphones, tablets. This is all using something called a Basic Service Set, or BSS. That is the idea that this access point is sitting there individually serving up clients in our home or small office. The BSS ID, the Basic Service Set ID, here is the MAC address of our wireless access point. Because we're using Ethernet here, our access point is going to have a MAC address associated with it, and our clients are going to send their traffic to that MAC address. The SSID is the Service Set Identifier, or the Service Set ID. The SSID, that's the name of our wireless network. When you visit your friend's house and they say, hey, what's your Wi-Fi network? You're telling them the name of the SSID here. In order to make this work, our wireless access point is almost always using something called an omnidirectional antenna, meaning that that antenna sends out a signal in virtually every direction uniformly. It can't do that perfectly. However, the idea of the omnidirectional antenna is that we send out the signal as uniformly as we possibly can based on the limitations of physics involved with using electromagnetic signals. A contrast to that is a point-to-point wireless network, which is going to use a directional antenna. Directional antennas just really aim the signal at a very small range. And that way, we can get a very powerful signal to go a pretty big distance. That way, if we have two buildings that are a couple miles apart or a couple of kilometers apart, what we can do is we can connect those two buildings together with a wireless network instead of installing fiber optics between these buildings or purchasing some service from an ISP. The idea here is that the antennas will send out a signal to each other, and they'll receive that and be able to do communication between these two buildings. One of the problems though is that with wireless networks, if you put something in the middle between it, you're going to interrupt the wireless signal, and it's not going to work quite as well. I worked for an organization once, and we have this exact setup where we had two buildings with directional antennas on the roof. We had them connected together, but every spring, the tree would get its leaves again, and it would grow a little bit taller, and it would interrupt that wireless signal. The users in one of the buildings would always complain that they would lose their network access, so we ended up having to put fiber optic to the building eventually. When we're using wireless networks to connect buildings together like this to do WAN connections between buildings, we have to pay attention to make sure that nobody's going to construct another building or there's not trees growing there. The main solution for this is something like a Yagi directional antenna. It looks like this image here.

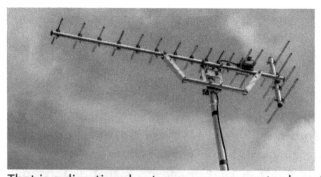

That is a directional antenna we can use to do point-to-point networks for wireless. Another way you can do this at home, if you want to build a home wireless network with a point-to-point network, you can find specifications to build something called a cantenna. You can actually use a Pringles can to make a wireless network and wireless point-to-point network to send signals between each other. You can do this for very inexpensively, just a few dollars to make this cantenna network. If you have a larger property and you're trying to get wireless networks between them, you might want to look at something like a Pringles cantenna out on the internet and see if you can build it to make a point-to-point wireless network. Wireless signal strength and quality are very important when we're talking about wireless networks. We measure our signal strength in decibels, which is labelled dB. Our signal strength is measured in decibels, and then we have something called a signal-to-noise ratio, and we really want the highest signal-to-noise ratio we can get. We want a lot of signal and not a lot of noise. What I mean by this is that if we have a wireless network, especially a 2.4 GHz wireless network, and this access point is sending out its signal, that signal can be interfered with by other devices, especially microwaves. A microwave also operates at 2.4 GHz. The reason is that at 2.4 GHz, that will resonate with a water molecule and actually make a water molecule spin around. When we put food in the microwave, there's water in the food, and we can spin those water molecules around, which then rub up against the other stuff in the food, and that heats up the food. It creates friction inside the food. The microwave oven is actually cooking the food from inside the food. The heat is generated from inside. When we turn on that microwave though, it sends out a massive, super loud, uncontrolled 2.4 GHz wireless signal, which ends up as being noise. When that happens here, you can kind of see my signal disappearing and reappearing. That would mean that the signal-to-noise ratio is very low, meaning there's lots of noise and not a lot of signal, which means that we can't actually use that signal, then to send and receive traffic. Sometimes if you're standing near a microwave when it's on, you may lose your wireless network capabilities. Another thing we can do here is something called wireless channel bonding. In our 2.4 GHz wireless spectrum, we had 22 MHz wide channels, and we could use channels 1, 6, and 11. One of the things we might do here is take channels 1 and 6 at 22 MHz each and combine them together into a 44 MHz channel. That would allow us to send on channel 1, we could send 54 megabits, on channel 6, we could send 54 megabits. When we combine them together, we can actually get a combined 108 megabits of throughput between our two devices. Wireless channel bonding allows us to take multiple channels, bond them together to get enhanced throughput between our devices.

## Chapter 19 Wireless Topologies and Management

Now let's take a look at topologies and management of wireless networks. There's several different wireless topologies we can set up. We can set up an ad hoc wireless network. This is used very rarely. We can set up a mesh network. Those can be used especially in outdoor environments. We can use wireless mesh networks, and we can have infrastructure wireless networks. A mesh wireless network is something that we would use when maybe we're setting up Wi-Fi in the city, and we're setting it up on the city streets for outdoor use. We can put access points on telephone poles and city streetlights. The access points themselves won't need a separate network connection going to them because what we'll do is we'll actually use a wireless mesh, meaning that those wireless access points on the telephone pole, they can connect to wireless clients walking along the street. They can also communicate with other wireless access points to provide them network access. The infrastructure mode is what we're going to use inside of our home networks, inside of our business networks. Ad hoc wireless networks use something called the Independent Basic Service Set. They typically are small Wi-Fi networks. They're used for sharing files and whatnot, used for toys or other electronic gadgets. I have a GoPro camera, and I can connect to it via an ad hoc wireless network in order to transfer the video files off of the GoPro onto my laptop. Sometimes toys will set up many Wi-Fi networks as well so that you can communicate with them or set them up or control them. Infrastructure wireless networks here are going to use something called an Extended Service Set. That home network we talked about used a Basic Service Set, and it was just a single access point with a single infrastructure on it so that we could connect our wireless devices to that single AP. In an enterprise network, we're going to use something called an Extended Service Set, an ESS. And that is used in enterprise Wi-Fi networks. Here we use that because typically in Wi-Fi networks in big businesses or bigger businesses, we're going to have more than one access point that we need to configure. We don't want to have a separate SSID for every single access point. With ESS, it allows us to have many, many, many access points, all operating on different channels, all using the same SSID. That way, I can roam around to different access points and never lose my network connection. In order to configure all these access points, we use something called a wireless LAN controller. With that, I would, as an administrator, I would go on to the wireless LAN controller, create some profiles that would push out the config to multiple access points. This is relative to the way you would do it at home. At home, you would connect directly to your access point typically and configure that access point individually. We used to do this in wireless networks for business. However, there became so many access points, this became very, very difficult to do. We went to this controller-based model where we can create profiles that we can send out to access points, and it allows us to give different services to different areas of our network. We also want to be able to roam around. Maybe we have a warehouse over there on the left and there's some people moving around there constantly and then inside the rest of the office, you know, maybe we have users that are going to move from their office and they might move into a conference room at some point. All this means that we have to provide enough wireless access to our devices so that as these users roam around, they have continuous access to a wireless network. We might do something like a wireless site survey to determine where our access points need to be placed in order to provide the coverage so that we can roam around our office building or a warehouse or wherever we're at and have continuous coverage of Wi-Fi to keep our users happy.

## Chapter 20 Wireless Encryption

Let's now talk about wireless encryption. The need for wireless encryption comes from this. Wireless is not like a wire, of course, it's not. If I plug my device into a wire, the only two devices that can hear that traffic is the device that's sending the traffic and the device that I'm sending it to. That might be a switch and the switch might be connected to a router, but I would have to be a device on that network to somehow received the traffic. With wireless, I don't have to be connected to the network, I don't even have to be inside of the house or the business that's sending out the wireless signal. I can do something called wardriving, which is driving around with a laptop searching for wireless networks that I can break into. If I can break into the wireless network and get connected to it, then I can see a lot of the traffic that's being sent and received on that wireless network. I can capture it and examine it and see if I can gather any useful or sensitive information. Wardriving is not a legal activity; however, it can be done and it's difficult to detect. I'm certainly not encouraging you to do that, I'm just saying this exists and it's the reason why we need to encrypt our wireless networks. Early encryption, especially on 802.11b, we used something called WEP, wired equivalency protocol, and the name is kind of a joke now. The idea was is that they were going to make this wireless encryption so that it would be the same as being connected to a wired network. But by 2002 or so, utilities existed to be able to crack the password used for WEP within seconds. You could capture the wireless password or the pre-shared key here, using WEP you could capture it in a matter of seconds and break into somebody's network. We needed to abandon WEP very quickly, which is where we came out with WPA, or Wifi Protected Access. This used one of two types of encryption in order to accomplish the goal. One was TKIP, which is Temporal Key Integrity Protocol and that was basically an extension of WEP. As we made the migration, we had to write software and update our hardware in order to accomplish the new encryption standard. But in order to make it a little bit backward compatible, we implemented TKIP, which is very similar to WEP, and actually is kind of easy to decrypt our key used to encrypt our data. That's why we would prefer to use AES, or the Advanced Encryption Standard protocol, for our encryption. So WPA supported both of these, TKIP as a backward compatibility type thing, and AES as our more sophisticated, and preferred encryption standard. Over time though, WPA also was easy to crack, the way it was implemented, so we implemented WPA2. WPA2 is Wifi Protected Access 2, and it also does both TKIP and AES but has additional mechanisms built into the protocol to make it much more difficult to crack the password used in order to encrypt our data. AES and WPA, we don't want to use those on any of our networks anymore unless we absolutely have to. Sometimes in medical environments or manufacturing environments the equipment we're using was either made to survive an extended period of time, you know,

10 years or more, or it was certified by some body like the FDA in the United States that allows that medical gear to be used in a hospital. When they do that, sometimes they have to certify it with very specific hardware that may not be capable of advanced encryption options. In those cases, we create firewalled networks in order to protect that equipment as much as we can. When we have the opportunity, we want to use a minimum of WPA2 encryption. When we're talking about that, we definitely don't want to use our TKIP option anymore, unless again we absolutely have to, we want WPA2 using AES encryption. There are two flavors here of WPA2 that we can use, one is personal, this is what we would use at home with a pre-shared key. When somebody comes into your home and they say, what's your wireless network? You tell them and then they say, okay, I need the passcode, that's the pre-shared key you're giving them, the PSK. You configure that on your wireless equipment. The second option here is enterprise version of WPA2. With enterprise, we're using a protocol called 802.1x. 802 is the Ethernet stuff protocols. 802.1x is an authentication protocol at Layer 2 that we can use to authenticate a user or some other method onto our network. This is going to use in wireless something called EAP-TLS in order to achieve that authentication. With that, we can use a username and password, we can also use something called a certificate. A certificate, we can generate a very specific certificate for a specific device, like a laptop or a smartphone. We can install that certificate on the device and then when we try to

connect to our wireless network using WPA2 in enterprise mode, we can send that certificate and say, hey, here's my certificate, I'm authentic, authenticate me. The wireless network will then say, this is legitimate, you're authenticated. Or if the certificate isn't valid, maybe it expired or maybe it was removed from the allowed certificates from the 802.1x system, then it would say reject that connection, not allow the wireless client to connect. In enterprise businesses is very useful because then we're not giving everyone the same pre-shared key, we can add or remove devices from the network or add or remove users from the network as we need to. If a user gets fired, we want to invalidate their username and password and prevent them from getting on the wireless network. If we had a pre-shared key, we'd have to change that pre-shared key and give it to everybody again, and that would make a messy situation. WPA3 is the latest version of WPA and that really is just using AES encryption and it's using just more bits of AES encryption, so it's slightly more secure, slightly more difficult to attack.

## Chapter 21 Cellular Wireless

Cellular wireless came in many different flavors over the years, and we start it off, specifically, when we talk about data networks in cellular wireless, it's evolved quite a bit over the last 20 years. The original versions of cellular all used analog-based connections. They were a poor connection, they didn't do a great job with even the voice traffic, and they didn't have a huge range. Later on, we went to digital cellular communication, and that allowed us a lot more options; although, our data capabilities on that were very, very, very limited. That was, up until we came out with this TDMA, or Time Division Multiple Access. TDMA was the type of cellular technology that allowed us to transfer data, but it allowed it at a very slow speed. This was the technology available when the iPhone first came out in 2007. Then we came out with GSM, the Global System for Mobile Communications. This standard was used generally around the world. In the United States it was only used on one or two carriers. GSM allowed for faster speed communications between devices, and a competing model to this was CDMA, or Code Division Multiple Access. GSM and CDMA were used by different carriers. GSM was used by AT&T and T-Mobile in the United States. CDMA was used by a lot of small carriers in the U.S. and Verizon Wireless. CDMA was used a lot more in the United States than it was used in the rest of the world. GSM was the primary technology there. Then we moved on to LTE, or Long-Term Evolution. LTE could make use of either CDMA-type technology or GSM-type technology to achieve higher data rates. LTE is still very popular around the world, and we're slowly moving on from it though. TDMA, that was a 2G wireless cellular network. GSM was considered 3G, or third generation. CDMA, also 3G. LTE is our 4G network. Then, now we're using LTE, the Long-Term Evolution, to also move on to 5G networks. 5G networks generally are still using the same technology as the LTE, we're just changing how the infrastructure operates on the back end to achieve a much lower latency, high-speed network. We are making some use of some new frequencies in 5G networks; however, those are typically for big cities versus other applications of this. In summary we've talked about the basics of wireless and discussed the physics or the physical layer of wireless and how we make use of wireless channels in the electromagnetic spectrum. We then moved on and talked about the data link layer component of this with 802.11 protocols and technologies like multiple input, multiple output, OFDMA, among other things. We talked about encrypting wireless, how we want to use WPA2 or WPA3 to encrypt our wireless networks. We wrapped it all up by talking about the different cellular technologies we use to transfer data. I hope this gives you a great introduction to wireless networks, specifically wireless Ethernet and those 802.11 protocols. Those are going to be very useful. All those terms are going to be very useful for you in your career in IT and in data networking.

## Chapter 22 Layer 2 Devices and Services

We're going to talk about modems, then we're going to talk about traffic shaping and see how we can give certain traffic priority on our network, and last, we're going to look at neighbor discovery protocols and see how those are relevant in our networks. These are all Layer 2 protocols that we're working with - Layer 2 stuff. A modem itself stands for modulator-demodulator. The original modems that we would use were actually a device that we would put on our telephone line and hook it into our computer in order to get some type of networked service. Initially, that was to a bulletin board service, or a BBS, which allowed us a text-based menu to transfer files and maybe do some chatting, maybe play some text-based games. All that modem did was it took a signal that the computer could understand, and it converted it into sounds and screeches and whatnot, that it was able to send that data connection over the phone line itself. It was a very slow operation. However, the modem eventually evolved into providing us internet connectivity in our homes. It's very likely that you have a device like this in your home if you have some type of wired internet service in your home or your business. This device provides wireless access. It also provides some wired Ethernet access, but then it also has an interface to connect back to the internet service provider. This device is converting a signal that's Ethernet that our computers and our phones can understand, and it's converting it into a signal that the internet service provider can understand. Here is a cable modem that I have an image of here. The cable modem, what it's doing is it's taking a protocol, a Layer 2 protocol called DOCSIS, which is Data Over Cable Service

Interface Specification, so it's the protocol that's used to transfer data over a cable TV wire over that coax cable.

DOCSIS is the connection that goes to the cable company. Ethernet is what we're going to use in our internal home network. So this device, this cable modem, is converting DOCSIS to Ethernet for us. Another type of modem we can have is a fiber optic modem. This is more of a media converter than it is a modem, even though we'll likely refer to this as a modem. The fiber optic modem, the media converter here, what we're doing is we're taking fiber optic Ethernet connections, and we're converting it into copper Ethernet connections. This device that we get from our internet service provider has a fiber optic port that we plug the fiber optic into, and that connects back to the internet service provider, and it converts it into copper Ethernet, which we can plug our devices into or plug a wireless access point into or some other type of Ethernet connection. These modems that we get from our internet service provider are usually a little bit more sophisticated than just being a Layer 2 media converter. It often has other options on it like firewalls to help protect our internal systems from the ugliness that exists on the internet. But the idea generally, is that this fiber optic modem from our internet service provider is just converting our fiber optic Ethernet into copper Ethernet. Another type of modem here is a DSL modem, or a digital subscriber line modem. These were very popular in the late 90s, early 2000s before the cable infrastructure was completed and certainly before we had any fiber objects into our homes. The DSL modem is digital subscriber line. It runs over our telephone wires. The telephone wires that are in our homes that give us land phone lines, if we still have a land phone line, we can use those land phone lines to provide internet service via DSL. DSL used audio, but the audio is outside of the range of human hearing. We were able to put specialized equipment in our central offices of the telephone companies, as well as use a DSL modem to provide higher speed internet access at like a megabit or 2 Mbps per second. It was relatively slow for modern standards, which means that this is actually antiquated now. We don't use this very much anymore. However, in maybe rural environments or in areas of the world where we don't have access to fiber optics or high speed wireless or cell infrastructure or cable modems, we might be using DSL infrastructure. The DSL modem here is typically converting the DSL signal, the digital subscriber line protocol that's used over the phone line to communicate to the internet service provider, it's converting that from DSL to Ethernet. That's what the purpose of this particular modem is.

## Chapter 23 Traffic Shaping

Traffic shaping is very useful when we have some traffic that needs high priority and definitely needs to get across the network quickly, versus traffic that can have a little bit more latency involved, it doesn't have to be prioritized at all. The distinction here is a distinction between making a phone call using voice over IP, which uses the data network, versus streaming a video from YouTube. For streaming a video from YouTube, YouTube can slowly gather the video, slowly download the video, and it can cache it in our browser so that when we hit play we get a nice continuous stream of video, we don't really have to worry about if there's latency on the network. A voice over IP call though, that's happening real time and live, and if we drop a packet, we don't get that packet later, it just doesn't show up at all, so we miss part of the conversation. Let's take a look at how we can use traffic shaping to our advantage here. Let's say I have two networks here.

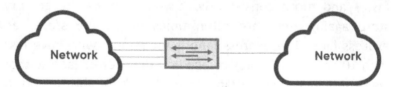

Here's two clouds with some network in it, and those networks are sending some traffic. As that traffic reaches the switch, by default, the switch is going to process the traffic in a first come, first serve basis. Just like you're going to the grocery store and you get into one of the lines at the grocery store, it's first come, first serve. There's no priority based on your status, or how many groceries you have, or anything like that, you get into the line that's available first come, first served. Well, if we do that same demonstration, but we use voice over IP here, we're going to pay attention this time to the messages at the top, which are coming from the phone.

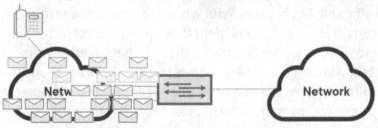

With first come, first serve here, we want the phone messages at the very top of that group of messages, we want those to flow in a nice stream. But if we process that first come, first serve, we have this huge delay before we get another message of our voice call on to that wire, so there's these delays as we're putting messages onto the wire and processing it through the switch. So, when we have voice over IP traffic, we definitely don't want our traffic to be prioritized first come, first serve. We really want our voice over IP traffic to have definite priority and get onto the wire faster and more consistently. If you think of the grocery store again, there are often times in grocery stores an express lane. The express lane is for people who have less than 10 or 15 items, they can go into the express lane so that we're not in the same lane of traffic where the person in front of me has two grocery carts full of food that needs to check out when I only have two things in my hand. That way I can go to the express lane and check out there. Here if we introduce traffic shaping, now what we can do is we can take those voice over IP messages coming from our phone and we can give them a special queue. So now whatever I send a message onto the wire, every other message is my voice over IP message, and that way, as I'm talking on the phone, those messages coming out of my phone are very nicely, neatly spaced on the wire and we can guarantee them priority when they are transferring over the wire. It's a matter of how we prioritize this traffic. The way we can do that is we can either add a special code into our header information, or we can configure our switch to give priority to certain VLANs over other VLANs. With traffic shaping, it's really a form of bandwidth management. We can do this in lots of different ways, for voice over IP calls we want to give those messages priority. In the sense of other traffic shaping though, we can do some bandwidth management where maybe we purchase a 50 megabit internet connection over a fiber optic cable from our internet service provider. Well, 50 megabits, there is no 50 megabit Ethernet, there's 100 megabit Ethernet, there's a gigabit Ethernet, there's 10 gigabit Ethernet, but no 50. So what we can do with that is we can actually do some bandwidth management similar to the way we do prioritization of traffic for voice over IPs. We can actually limit the amount of bandwidth allowed on a link, that's one method we can use here. We can implement quality of service, and that's really what we're doing with traffic shaping when we're talking about voice over IP calls, or video calls, or other types of services, maybe emergency services that require a high level of priority on the data network. Flow control is another way of implementing quality of service. That's something that we can implement on our switches to allow for traffic to be sent efficiently and effectively.

## Chapter 24 Neighbor Device Discovery

Now, let's talk about neighbor discovery, which is another layer two function on our network. When we have a bunch of networked devices, like routers and switches, sometimes even firewalls, it's very easy to get lost in the mess of cabling and connections. So here's a very simple network.

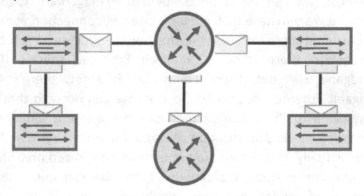

What neighbor discovery does is it sends out messages at layer two, very simple messages, and it says, hey, I'm a router, I have these capabilities and this is the port that I'm sending this message out on, and then the device that's listening for that message says, oh great, thanks, I'm going to add that to my table, and it sends back the same kind of information to the other device. This only happens with neighboring devices. Not all the devices see all the traffic, that would make a mess of our network. The idea here is that we want to see who is directly connected to us. This is an outstanding tool for troubleshooting networks when we are uncertain what devices are connected, or maybe we have some unusual behavior happening, maybe a cable did not get reconnected correctly. What we can use is we can use these neighbor discovery protocols then to learn about our neighbors, and the idea here is that if we take a look at this router in the middle, that router is going to learn about its neighbors through neighbor discovery protocol, its neighbors are going to be the switch on the left and the right, and the router on the bottom. In the table on this router, we could look at that table by issuing a command and it would say, there's a switch attached to the left, there's a switch attached to the right, there's a router attached below you, and these are the capabilities of that device. If we take a look at the switch over on the upper left, that's going to learn about the router and the switch that are directly connected to it. If we look at the router on the bottom, that's only going to learn about the router on the top and no other devices, and if we take a look at the switch on the bottom right, that's only going to learn about the switch that's directly connected to it and no other devices. When we're looking at neighbor discovery protocols here, there's two that we generally use. One is Link Layer Discovery Protocol. This is for devices that are not Cisco based. The other one is CDP, or Cisco Discovery Protocol. CDP is prevalent on all Cisco devices, it is typically enabled by default, so we're able to see the devices that are directly connected to each other. I've actually seen non-Cisco devices even using CDP, it's a pretty simple protocol, it's so widely deployed, it's very useful in discovering what network devices are directly connected to ourselves. This makes, again, tremendous use when we're doing troubleshooting, it can introduce a layer of potential security issue, because if somebody attaches to our device that is not authorized, they can look at this information from our neighbor discovery and learn more about our network, quickly. Most organizations value the troubleshooting capabilities of this over the potential security risks, though. In summary we took a look at modems and saw the difference between three types of modems: a cable modem, a fiber optic modem, a DSL modem; and we learned that they're really doing some type of media conversion from one layer 2 protocol to another layer 2 protocol. We looked at traffic shaping and saw how we can take VoIP traffic and prioritize it on the network by giving it a special queue, and then last, we took a look at neighbor discovery protocol. Neighbor discovery protocol allows us to see our directly connected network devices that we're using. I hope this was valuable to see some layer 2 devices. Next we're going to take a look at other network devices that are important to network infrastructure; however, they didn't necessarily fit into the other categories.

## Chapter 25 Load Balancer Fundamentals

Now, we're going to talk about other networked devices that we couldn't fit into the other parts of this book. First, we're going to take a look at load balancers and see what they do. We'll look at firewalls and see some different firewall options we have. We're going to talk a little bit about voice over IP, and then we'll talk about some other networked devices that we may find on our network that need IT support. First, let's start with load balancers. A load balancer is going to operate typically between the network layer and the transport layer. We may have some application layer functions here as well. What a load balancer does, so first of all, here is the icon that represents a load balancer, and what a load balancer does is it is a device that sits in the network and allows us to have a single IP address called a VIP, or a virtual IP address.

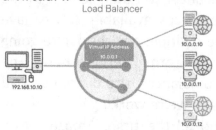

Here, my virtual IP address is 10.0.0.1, and then that is going to connect to several different servers. Here I have three different servers, 10.0.0.10, 10.0.0.11, and 10.0.0.12. The whole purpose of our load balancer is to have numerous servers that can all respond to requests from clients simultaneously. What this does is it distributes the load across numerous devices. If we have a very popular website, we can put that website on three or more different web servers, and then use a load balancer so that when the client connects to it, the client is actually going to connect to IP address 10.0.0.1. When we have our DNS entry, our DNS entry is going to have the website that we're going to, and it's going to map to 10.0.0.1 here. Then when that traffic from my workstation gets to the load balancer, it will direct the traffic to the server that has the lowest load or whatever policy we implement on that load balancer to make a decision of which server to send it to. A lot of time, this will be done round-robin, meaning it will send the first request to the first server, the second one to the second, the third one to the third, and then the fourth one back to the first, and so on. Another way we might do this is the load balancer may send out a health check, asking each server how many resources are available, and the load balancer will then send it to the server with the most resources available. If we have multiple devices here, the multiple devices, we're going to send additional traffic to other servers here. The whole purpose of the load balancer is to distribute load over multiple servers. When we're working in the cloud, this happens in the cloud all the time. Amazon Web Services or Google or Microsoft Azure all have these load balancer services available. It allows them to spin up additional servers to handle additional network traffic from their customers. So load balancers are a critical component in modern networks.

## Chapter 26 Firewall Fundamentals

Firewalls are a security device. Traditional firewalls operate at the transport layer.

The idea of the firewall is that we want to keep our traffic inside our network, we want to keep that safe and secure, and we don't want the internet traffic getting in. The internet is kind of like a Wild, Wild West of traffic, and almost anything can pass on the internet as just IP packets. We don't want anybody to be able to get access to our network, so we set up a firewall, and part of the purpose of the firewall is it lets traffic from the inside of the network out, but it doesn't let outside traffic back in, unless somebody from the inside sent it. We do this with a series of features with access control lists where we're limiting IP addresses or a range of IP addresses and port numbers or a range of port numbers. Sometimes we want people from the internet to get into our network, and when we do that, we set up a special area in the network called a DMZ, effectively named after the military version of this, the demilitarized zone. The DMZ, what it does is it allows us to have servers and other services on devices in the DMZ, and it allows us to create a special access control list or a filter that allows certain traffic from the internet to come into our inside network, access the services needed in the DMZ, and then return back to the internet. This is the whole purpose of our firewall here is to really act as a secure boundary between our inside networks, our internet networks, and our DMZ or secured networks. Not all firewalls operate at the transport layer. Modern firewalls or next-generation firewalls here, actually operate at the application layer, and they're going to do more than just operate at the application layer; they're also going to operate at the transport and network layers, too. It's going to have the same type of services available as a traditional firewall where we can filter traffic based on IPs and port numbers. However, in addition to that, it's going to include something called intrusion detection or intrusion prevention. These are an IDS and IPS device as well, intrusion detection system or intrusion prevention system. What's happening here is our next-generation firewall has a database built into it, and the database that's built into it has a bunch of signatures of malicious traffic or of traffic that's undesirable in our network. What the IDS/IPS system is doing is it's watching. Every single message that passes through our firewall is inspected against this database to see if it matches the signature of not desirable traffic. If it matches that signature, what we can do is we can either just automatically throw that message away, that would be intrusion prevention, or we can send an alert to an administrator saying, hey, there's some nefarious activity happening on our firewall, we should go investigate it, here's the device that's sending it. This can happen in both directions. If our computer on the inside of our network gets a virus and it starts sending out traffic that's not standard, we can recognize that and take action. Another thing that the next-generation firewall might do is have something called a proxy server or a content filter. A proxy server allows us to filter web and other internet traffic so that our users can only access information that's valuable, at least that's valuable to the business. We can program that proxy server to allow certain content and block other content. In companies I've worked for, they have blocked Facebook, so they don't want their employees looking at Facebook during the day. Other organizations I've worked for have blocked Craigslist and other things like that so people can't shop during the day, so eBay and Craigslist are blocked. A lot of times, managers like to use the proxy server to manage their staff instead of actually having to go talk to and encourage their employees to do quality work. We use the proxy server to actually block traffic. Sometimes a proxy server is extra important in that maybe we're trying to protect intellectual property, design ideas, and maybe a new release of a product that we don't want to get leaked out into the world, that proxy server can help us filter the places where those events might happen and actually prevent some of that. Another option we have on our firewalls is something called a VPN concentrator. A VPN concentrator, or another word for this is a VPN headend, is it allows external users to gain access to services on the inside of the network when they're not at work. VPN concentrators and VPN headends became a critical piece of infrastructure during the pandemic, and what they allowed is it allowed people to work from home and access networked resources in their offices from their home computers. The idea here is that the users have an internet connection at home, and they can build a connection using a VPN from their workstation to this VPN concentrator and allow them access to internal resources. A VPN is a virtual private network, and what it does is it creates a type of tunnel through the internet, and that tunnel is really nothing more than putting IP packets inside of other IP packets and then moving it across the internet, and while those packets are inside packets are also encrypted, so nobody can see what's happening. This allows us to give users access to very specific resources inside of our network without compromising security. Another type of firewall that we can have here is a unified threat management device, and this is basically a next-generation firewall. It's going to be a layer 7 firewall or application layer firewall. These firewalls can pay attention to specific applications. Instead of just looking at a port number, like a traditional firewall, layer 7 or application layer firewalls, next-generation firewalls, all of them can actually look and see, oh, this is HTTP traffic, let's make sure that the person trying to access HTTP is actually doing it from a web browser that's valid versus trying to form some type of attack into our network and tricking the firewall into thinking it's going to a website, but really it's launching an attack. This UTM device also can do content filtering and proxy server, it can also do IDS/IPS. This layer 7 unified threat management firewall, these devices are very useful in helping prevent malicious traffic from getting onto your network, as well as detecting malicious traffic and other types of network attacks that are happening inside your network. You can take action a lot faster.

## Chapter 27 VoiP & SCADA Systems

There was a time 20 years ago and Voice over IP was a fad or appeared to be a fad, and now it is pretty much standard across the board of how we make voice phone calls inside of a business. Voice over IP is where we have a phone, and the phone has a switch in it that we connect to the network. I've talked about this before when we had a voice VLAN and a data VLAN, and we actually plug our PC right into our phone. Here I just have our phone shown. It's connected to the network. We'll give the traffic on that phone priority on our network using some type of quality of service. And then that phone is going to connect to something called a VoIP gateway.

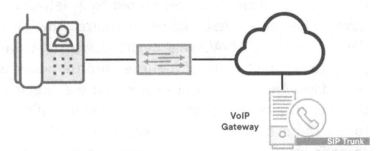

VoIP
Gateway

SIP Trunk

The VoIP gateway is going to be the device that handles all the incoming and outgoing phone calls. It's going to be the device that makes your phone ring. It's going to be the device that, when you dial a phone number, you're sending a message to the VoIP gateway, and then it's going to use something called a SIP trunk to connect to the plain old telephone service or our telephone service provider. It's going to allow multiple phone calls to happen simultaneously over that data network connection, that SIP trunk. Our VoIP gateway is going to be responsible for actually dialing the phone over that SIP trunk so we can get somebody's phone in some other location to ring. In Voice over IP, we have our VoIP phone, we're going to use quality of service, and it's all going to connect to this VoIP gateway. Let's look at some other devices for enterprise networks that you might encounter. Some of these are pretty common sense like printers. Inside of your network, you're going to have a printer connected to the data network. Printers may not necessarily be a smart device, but it's going to fall in this category of other networked devices. HVAC. This is one you may not think about is being networked, but our thermostats and other controllers for our heating, ventilating, and air conditioning equipment is likely to be connected to a network and have some server that's going to control how all the devices operate. HVAC is a smart device that we're going to see a lot more of in our enterprise businesses nowadays. Another type of device that we're going to see is physical access controls or card readers. It's going to be some device that we use, maybe it's a palm scanner, maybe it's a retina scanner, but it's most likely going to be some type of card that you're issued at your organization that you can use to scan on a keypad or scan on a card reader that will open doors for you, or it may give you access to certain devices. These are all typically networked together in modern systems. In modern security systems, we're going to use these card readers, and they're going to be connected to a data network. Another one we might see is Internet of Things devices. These might be smart lightbulbs, smart speakers, thermostats, refrigerators, doorbells, all kinds of things. A lot of these things were going to see in our homes. However, Internet of Things devices are becoming more popular in enterprise networks as well. The reason for this is that they're small, and they can collect a lot of data. Another type of device is a security camera that's going to be connected to our data network. A lot of new security cameras now are all IP-based. They might even connect over the wireless network. Security cameras are another type of device that we're going to see on our data network that we need to accommodate. One last one here and this one's a little bit strange. This is industrial controls. Industrial controls and SCADA systems, the SCADA stands for supervisory control and data acquisition. These are devices that we use in a factory, and a lot of them have been used for quite a long time actually where manufacturing data can actually be sent to and collected by a central server. Then that information is used to figure out how to make the machines work better or adjust their performance and whatnot. These industrial controls or SCADA controls, these are very, very, very important in manufacturing. A lot of these require some specialized security because they are more easily attacked because a lot of them are a little bit more antiquated, and they weren't ready for modern network use. These security controls are smart devices in our systems that we use that are going to be connected to the network. They're typically going to require extra special security to prevent them from being attacked. We have printers, HVAC equipment, security cameras, card readers, IoT things, SCADA devices. These are all types of devices that we're likely to see on our network that require special attention in order to get configured properly. In summary we talked about load balancers, and we saw how load balancers can distribute traffic to multiple servers to make sure that end users have a quality experience. We took a look at firewalls and took a look at both Layer 4 firewalls and Layer 7 firewalls, as well as IDS, IPS and proxy servers. We looked at voice over IP and saw how the voice over IP gateway is the central server for making and receiving voice phone calls. Then we looked at other networked devices that we may see in our networks. I hope you enjoyed this book and learned a lot about data network devices and how they operate. Routers and switches are such a critical component of IT, especially data networking, and understanding their operation is very, very important.

## Chapter 28 Network Monitoring

First we're going to cover network monitoring and talk about how we use network monitoring to pay attention to our network status. We're going to talk about the need for network monitoring, second, we're going to talk about some network monitoring details, and then we're actually going to observe a real network monitoring server. This is one that you can download for free. It is a bit sophisticated to set up, so we're going to look at a few of the features on it and talk a little bit more about what is entailed with network monitoring and why we use it. In our business network, we're going to have lots of devices in our network. There's going to be switches, and routers, and layer 3 switches, servers and there's going to be redundant connections. The big reason we need network monitoring here is that should an event happen, like a link goes down, we want to know about it. Early on in my career, I worked for an organization and we had some relatively new fiber optic circuits - this was quite a while ago, and those new fiber optic circuits ran throughout the city and connected our buildings together. They were doing road construction on one of the roads near the fiber and actually the fiber optic got cut, and we did not have a good network monitoring solution set up. It didn't break our network, but it did break some redundancy, so we weren't even aware that this fiber optic link was down until months later when we tried to use it and it didn't work. We instantly turned on a network monitoring solution to make sure we knew about any links or devices that ever went down. What network monitoring does for us is it pays attention to our network, sends out little messages asking what the status is of all the different systems, and it allows us to alert when a device goes down or a link goes down, or something is generally broken in our network, like one of the devices starts on fire, or there's a fire in the data center that starts, and it breaks our devices. When there are issues in the network, a good network monitoring system set up with quality alerting will allow us to determine when we have issues in our network. Network monitoring is going to monitor performance metrics and some sensors of some of our gear to determine temperature. That's going to have information about interface statistics, so, how much data is passed through an interface, are there any errors, is the interface up or down? It can pay attention to, again, interface errors and alert on those errors, as well as environmental factors and sensors, so we can put sensors in our buildings to check the temperature, humidity as well as device uptime and downtime. Our network monitoring is going to tell us when the last time a device rebooted, so that if for some reason there was a power outage or maybe our UPS, our battery backup system, failed, we get an alert telling us that this device rebooted and we know how long it has been online. This can be a very effective troubleshooting tool.

## Chapter 29 Layer 2 Errors

There's different types of errors we can have with Ethernet. One of them is a giant, and a giant means that our Ethernet frame exceeds the MTU, so it's bigger than 1500 bytes by default. We can enable jumbo frames, and that will eliminate our error of giants. A giant is a message that's too large, and our switch will likely throw that away. A runt is a message that's too tiny. Something happened to the message, and it was too tiny, and it can't be processed, and that will show up as an error, and that message should probably be thrown away. There might be an encapsulation error. Maybe we are expecting a non-tagged frame, and we receive the tag frame, and it might show up as an encapsulation error. There's also something called a CRC error, and I've mentioned this before. This is a cyclical redundancy check, and this is part of the frame headers itself. Let's take a look at how that works. Frame check sequence. This is the field at the end of the frame, so it's the FCS field.

| Destination MAC Address | Source MAC Address | Type | Data (Packet) | FCS |
|---|---|---|---|---|
| 48 bits | 48 bits | 16 bits | MAX 1500 Bytes | 32 bits |

To calculate that field, we do something called a cyclical redundancy check, so here's how that works. We take the contents of the frame, everything except the FCS. It's going to be a bunch of 1s and 0s. We take those 1s and 0s that consist of our frame, and we run it through our CRC algorithm process. This is just a mathematical formula. We're taking the 1s and 0s in our frame. We're putting it through this process, and it spits out a 32-bit value. We take that 32-bit value, and we attach it to our frame by filling in our FCS field with that 32-bit value. We then take that frame, we send it across the wire. When we send it across the wire, that frame could get tampered with. Maybe not by an attacker, but maybe that wire or the cable is going past a fluorescent light or maybe there's some type of unwanted interference, and it may change a couple of the bits in the frame. Well, when the switch receives that frame, what it's going to do is it's going to do the same process again. It's going to take that frame. It's going to take everything except the FCS value, the 1s and 0s of our frame, it's going to run it through the same exact process. It's going to spit out another 32-bit value. We then compare the two 32-bit values. We calculated the 32-bit value before we sent the frame on the wire, then we calculated the value again when the switch received it, and now we compare them. If they are equal, then that's great. The frame passes. If for some reason they don't match and something happened with the frame along the way and they're not equal, that's bad, and we throw that frame away, and we let other protocols figure out that we need to resend that frame. These are going to show up in our network monitoring as errors, as CRC errors. We can go check out and see what's happening with those errors and try to resolve that issue.

## Chapter 30 Facilities Monitoring

Another thing we can do with network monitoring is facilities monitoring. Facilities monitoring allows us to check on the places where we have data networking gear. Facilities monitoring, we're going to be checking things like the building or the room temperature. In a data center, we really don't want the temperature to get too high because we need to keep our servers cool. If our servers get too hot, the processors don't work as efficiently, or they just burn up. Another thing we might check is humidity. We don't want too much humidity in our data centers and in other facilities, so we're going to have some humidity control. These are checking our HVAC equipments' operational status. We might check electrical status as well. In data centers and in buildings where we're running a lot of IT gear, we usually have some redundant systems. We have battery backups. We have more than one source of power into the building ideally. What we would do is we'd have some monitoring set up to pay attention to see what's happening with that electrical system. Another thing we might pay attention for is is there a flood? We may have a sensor in our floors and in our buildings to make sure that nothing is flooding, and this happens from time to time. Either a rainstorm comes through, a water pipe bursts, some fire suppression has issues, and it may flood an area, and we really want to pay attention to that. In addition to monitoring the network with something like Observium, we can also use a program like Observium to collect data and monitor our facilities as well. This wraps up talking about what network monitoring is and taking a look at the server that we would use for that. We talked about the need for network monitoring. We want to make sure that we know what's happening on our network, especially for redundant links that might be hard to pay attention to if we're not looking. We took a look at network monitoring details and saw some of the things that we monitor like device uptime, CPU usage, link states, sent and received traffic, interface errors, and things like that. I hope this was valuable for you to get an understanding of network monitoring. Network monitoring is likely a tool that you will use as an entry-level network technician to pay attention and see what's happening on the network and see if anything needs attention. Next, I'm going to show you how we populate all of that network monitoring information in our server.

## Chapter 31 Collecting Network Monitoring & Baselining

Previously, we learned how critical network monitoring is to pay attention to what's happening with devices, and interfaces, and logs, and now we're going to take a look at how we collect that data to put into our network monitoring system. First, to talk about what baselining is. Then, we'll talk about SNMP, Simple Network Management Protocol, and then we'll move on to NetFlow and then logging and talk about different types of logging and severity levels. Baselining, what this means is we have all these devices in our network, and they are going to operate well under certain conditions. We design our network, we put the device in our network, and then if the devices meet the design criteria of our network, we should expect a nice even flow of operation. The processor utilization should be consistent. Memory utilization should be pretty consistent or have these little ups and downs as these devices process information. What we can do with our monitoring software is we can take this baseline, and the baseline basically is what's standard happening in our network. But what I'm talking about here is that our devices under normal conditions are going to exhibit a certain behavior, and we're going to watch for that behavior in our network monitoring software. Then what we can do as our network has processed data for a while, if we then see a spike in something, a spike in traffic, a spike in processor utilization, memory utilization, interface utilization, we can alert in our monitoring software that, hey, something is off of the baseline, and you should know about it and take action or at least investigate what's going on. Maybe a user started 15 10GB file transfers all at the same time and overwhelmed the link, and we can go talk to that user and find a solution for that user to actually reduce or modify how that user downloads data. Baselining is an important part of networking, and we're going to be doing that with our network monitoring software, and we're going to try to pay attention to these spikes in changes in our general use of our network.

## Conclusion

Congratulations on completing this book! I am sure you have plenty on your belt, but please don't forget to leave an honest review. Furthermore, if you think this information was helpful to you, please share anyone who you think would be interested of IT as well.

## About Richie Miller

Richie Miller has always loved teaching people Technology. He graduated with a degree in radio production with a minor in theatre in order to be a better communicator. While teaching at the Miami Radio and Television Broadcasting Academy, Richie was able to do voiceover work at a technical training company specializing in live online classes in Microsoft, Cisco, and CompTia technologies. Over the years, he became one of the top virtual instructors at several training companies, while also speaking at many tech and training conferences. Richie specializes in Project Management and ITIL these days, while also doing his best to be a good husband and father.